easy elegance

easy elegance

creating a relaxed, comfortable and stylish home

Atlanta Bartlett
photography by Polly Wreford

rps

RYLAND PETERS & SMALL
LONDON • NEW YORK

Senior designer Megan Smith
Commissioning editor Annabel Morgan
Location research Jess Walton
Production manager Patricia Harrington
Art director Leslie Harrington
Publishing director Alison Starling

First published in the UK in 2009
This paperback edition published in 2014 by
Ryland Peters and Small
20–21 Jockey's Fields
London WC1R 4BW
and
519 Broadway, 5th Floor
New York, NY 10012

www.rylandpeters.com

10 9 8 7 6 5 4 3 2 1

Text © Atlanta Bartlett 2009, 2014
Design and photographs
© Ryland Peters & Small 2009, 2014

ISBN: 978-1-84975-509-2

All rights reserved. No part of this
publication may be reproduced,
stored in a retrieval system or
transmitted in any form or by any
means, electronic, mechanical,
photocopying or otherwise,
without the prior permission
of the publisher.

A CIP record for this book is
available from the British Library.

Printed and bound in China

Library of Congress Cataloging-in-
Publication Data for the original book:

Bartlett, Atlanta.
  Easy elegance : creating a relaxed,
comfortable, and stylish home / Atlanta
Bartlett ; photography by Polly Wreford. --
1st ed.
    p. cm.
  Includes index.
  ISBN 978-1-84597-850-1
1. Interior decoration. 2. House
furnishings. I. Wreford, Polly. II. Title.
NK2115.B32 2009
747--dc22

                        2008047680

For David, whose love and inspiration
has made this book possible.

contents

introduction

When I started styling 20 years ago, there were really only four main interior design magazines on the market, but you only have to look at the newsstands today to appreciate how this area of interest has exploded in recent years. These days we are assailed by information overload. Television, radio, newpapers and billboards vie for our attention, laying down the law and offering advice on everything from how to bring up our children and conduct our relationships to what clothes we should wear and how we should decorate our homes. In the world of interiors, this has had a diluting effect on our personal tastes, as people try to conform to the style diktats of designers, magazine editors and high-street stores.

My own approach to decorating started as a backlash against the formality of interior-designed homes and the blanket of bland 'good taste' spreading across the shops. *Easy Elegance* is not so much a design principle as a way of life, with personal expression, comfort and practicality at its heart. It's about believing in your own taste and having the conviction to stick to it – after all, there is no such thing as the style police!

My appreciation of the imperfect, abhorrence of needless consumerism and love of time-worn things and functional design has slowly crystallized into a coherent style. Easy Elegance is the result of ideas that have developed in my mind over the years, with help and inspiration from my husband and partner, Dave Coote.

In this book I show you how to re-connect with your own personal style and create a home that works for you as an individual. The first section explains the four main elements of Easy Elegance: Comfort, Simplicity, Function, and Individuality. With these in place you can consider the mood you want to evoke in your home. In Setting the Scene, I map out five interpretations of the style so you can identify the one that most appeals, while remembering that you can pick and choose from any or all of them, if that's what suits you best. Choose from the clean lines of Modern Elegance, cosy and comforting Country Elegance, the quirky appeal of Retro Elegance, the soft sensuality of Feminine Elegance and the crumbling charm of Faded Elegance. And finally I take you through your home room by room, offering practical tips and easily achievable ideas, and showing you how to make this simple but beautiful philosophy work for you.

What is *easy* elegance?

Easy Elegance is not so much a design style as a way of life. It's a chic but relaxed look that rejects prescriptive style rules in favour of a more personal approach to decorating. Comfort, simplicity, function and individuality are the key ingredients of the look, and the result is a home that's warm and welcoming, yet versatile and smart.

MAKE YOUR HOME YOUR
COMFORT ZONE – CHOOSE
INVITING TEXTURES, SOOTHING
COLOURS AND FURNITURE
THAT INVITES YOU TO RELAX.

comfort

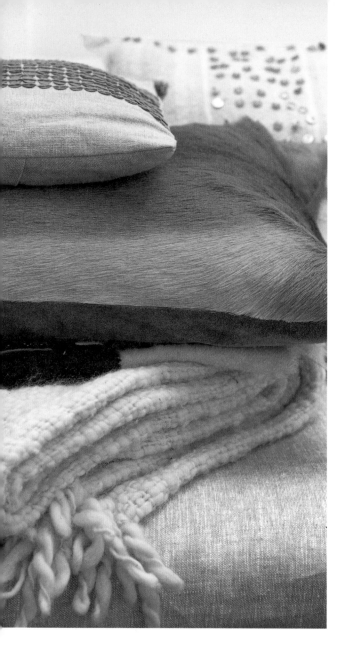

Home offers us a retreat from the daily hurly burly of life, and being comfortable at home is key to feeling relaxed and secure in general. Comfort can be introduced into your home in many ways: through texture, for sensuousness and intimacy; via colour, for warmth and stimulation; in furnishings, for the practicalities of day-to-day living; and by simply surrounding yourself with objects you love and enjoy.

Texture plays an important role in making us feel soothed and cosseted. Surrounding yourself with tactile fabrics and materials feeds both body and soul, whatever decorative style you are aiming for. Stone, wood, wool and animal skins can be layered for an earthy modern feel; while velvet, silk and lace will combine to create a sexy, feminine vibe. For a rustic mood, try mixing rough linen, chunky handknits, basketware and flagstones, or, if you lean more towards a smart urban look, team linen with cashmere, leather and glass.

Walls and floors can play a vital role in bringing texture into the home, and panelling the walls is a great way to create cosiness. Try horizontal cedarwood planks for a sleek contemporary look or traditional Georgian-style panelling for a classic effect. The versatile qualities of tongue-and-groove mean it can provide a backdrop in a variety of settings, including modern, country and beach houses. Panelling can also be used to change the proportions of a room. Limiting the height of the panels to dado- or to picture-rail level will make the ceilings

ABOVE Tactile fabrics in a variety of textures add sensuousness to an interior. Here, a Canadian horse blanket is teamed with a contemporary wool throw and cushions in animal skin and linen decorated with sequins.

RIGHT The eclectic mix of well-worn antiques, traditional panelling and retro details creates a cosy scheme that's reminiscent of a Scottish hunting lodge but with an edgy feel that brings it right up to date.

LEFT This opulent bedroom proves that glamour and comfort can go hand in hand. Heaps of cushions, made from remnants of furnishing fabrics and vintage clothes, are layered with plump eiderdowns and lengths of exotic sari silk to create a sumptuous boudoir effect that is both sexy and cosy.

ABOVE A soft colour scheme like this one, which combines warm shades of delicate pink with gold and strong magenta, creates a soothing ambience.

ABOVE White on white doesn't have to look cold and clinical if treated in the right way. Layer different textures to create a scheme with depth and warmth.

Stone, wood, wool and animal skins can be layered to create an earthy modern feel; while velvet, silk and lace combine to create a sexy, ultra-feminine vibe.

appear lower to create a more intimate feel, while panelling just a section of a room can create an inviting den-like corner.

Flooring should be both sensual and practical. Hardwood is pleasing to walk on and resilient, while limestone has a silky feel that tempts you to remove your shoes. Cheap pine floorboards are affordable and versatile, as they can be painted (and repainted) whatever colour takes your fancy.

Colour is a very personal thing and we are all naturally drawn to different palettes. However, rich, dark colours are an obvious choice when trying to evoke a sense of comfort and warmth. Teal walls, the warm chocolate of a worn leather

armchair, touches of gold and a dash of bright orange will combine to create the luxurious intimacy of a modern-day gentleman's club. The muted, mid-range tones of heritage colours such as smoky green, mahogany and stone possess a subtle, calming elegance, while neutrals like cream, almond or taupe don't demand attention, but allow the appreciation of texture and form. And the misconception that white is cold and clinical is quickly dispelled when it is layered in many different textures – crisp cotton, creamy lambskin, white plaster walls and limewashed floorboards – to create an all-white scheme that has warmth and depth.

LEFT A well-worn leather armchair is an inviting spot for a quiet read in this sunny corner.
BELOW Fluffy mohair throws and antique Welsh blankets in washed-out pastel shades will create a cosy feel that's also pretty and feminine.

A huge feather-filled sofa will make any room seem warm and inviting. Go for the best you can afford, although even the most modest model will be lifted into the realms of luxury when piled high with soft throws and outsized scatter cushions. Battered, well-worn furniture with a history has the familiarity of an old friend, and is a great way to create a comfortable but elegant look.

Squashy sofas, snug blankets and crisp cotton sheets are not the only things that will enhance a sense of wellbeing. Surround yourself with treasured possessions – a wall of black and white family photos, for example, will instantly personalize a room. If you mount and frame them properly, they will become a decorative feature in their own right. Personal touches such as this will give your home soul. Perhaps the one thing that soothes you after a hard day is curling up beneath an old blanket crocheted by your grandmother, but you worry that it's too shabby to be on display. Easy Elegance, however, is all about creating a home that meets your needs – a home that looks lived in as well as stylish. So instead of banishing that blanket to the cupboard under the stairs and only sneaking it out when you're on your own, embrace the comfort factor and make a quirky feature of it. Team it with something unexpected like a Moroccan leather footstool for a funky retro look, or throw it over a simple, beautiful, hand-crafted chair to create a pared-down country theme.

THIS PAGE This deceptively simple scheme is actually a sensory haven full of warmth, texture and contrast. An antique linen sheet, dyed charcoal grey, is strewn with satin and velvet cushions, a goatskin rug lies on bare boards, and side tables are ingeniously devised from upturned apple crates and a silver-birch log.

KEEP IT SIMPLE – AND YOU
WILL BRING A WELCOME
SENSE OF ORDER, CALM AND
SERENITY TO YOUR HOME.

simplicity

One of the key components of Easy Elegance is simplicity. In a world saturated with noise, information overload and rampant consumerism, simplicity offers a welcome antidote to our hectic modern existence, and the pared-down look has become synonymous with contemporary style. However, think beyond the clichéd minimalist interior of bare white walls and concrete floors, for Easy Elegance takes an altogether softer approach. Whatever your style – coolly modern, a mixture of old and new, relaxed country or faded grandeur – simplicity will bring a sense of calm and order that is key to Easy Elegance.

Simplicity is as much about exercising restraint as it is about making style choices, in that what you choose to leave out is every bit as important as what you choose to include. See your home as a blank canvas, a backdrop for your favourite possessions. Pare down the decorative elements

OPPOSITE LEFT This pared-down bedroom exudes monastic calm. An old metal factory stool serves as a bedside table.

OPPOSITE RIGHT This old marble-topped table is given a modern twist by being set against a rough, black-painted brick wall in a contemporary kitchen. The gas-powered candelabrum by Moooi is a fun and funky take on a traditional shape.

OPPOSITE BELOW A pile of pure and simple white ceramic kitchenware makes an impact.

RIGHT Treasured possessions, like these antique bowls, can be properly appreciated if the rest of the room is kept simple.

BELOW LEFT This monochrome kitchen shouts utilitarian chic. Sleek black-stained wood units are contrasted with an untreated concrete floor and galvanized-steel chairs for a no-frills look.

BELOW RIGHT Keeping all the elements in a room below eye level creates a refreshing sense of height and space.

OPPOSITE The curvaceous lines of a 1960s chair add organic shape to the straight lines of this bold black-on-black bathroom. **LEFT** Floor-to-ceiling concealed cupboards enable the owners of this serene, tranquil dining space to keep the area clutter-free. **BELOW** Low-level banquette seating emphasizes height and space. The ethnic details give the room warmth and individuality.

to just one or two outstanding pieces and instead concentrate on getting the basics right. Maximize natural light and space, choose practical yet stylish furniture, and exert self-control when it comes to the finishing touches.

A sense of space is fundamental. Not everyone is lucky enough to live in a vast converted warehouse, but whatever the size of your home there are tricks you can use to help create the illusion of space. Pale colours and neutrals pull in light, which makes a room feel bigger, so keep the walls, floors and furnishings an unobtrusive shade. Painting both the walls and the woodwork the same colour will also help – forcing architectural details to recede into the background enhances a feeling of spaciousness. And use optical illusions to play around with the proportions of the room. Low-level wall-to-wall shelving will bring your eye level down, making ceilings feel higher, while laying extra-long floorboards will create the illusion of an elongated floor area. Choosing leggy furniture or small-scale pieces also helps to increase a sense of space.

Simplicity is as much about exercising restraint as it is about making the right style choices.

In the pursuit of simplicity, resist the temptation to strip back the details and banish any traces of colour from your home. Bare walls and minimal furniture may sound seductively simple, but a clinical feel is not appropriate in an Easy Elegance home. Bear in mind that comfort and individuality should never be compromised, and some form of personal expression is indispensable. Don't feel that everything needs to match or ruthlessly rid yourself of items that don't fit into a particular scheme.

In order to create a sense of simplicity, all you need is cohesion, and this can be achieved by unifying several disparate elements. A mismatched array of sofas and armchairs of different ages can be pulled together by covering them all in loose covers/slipcovers made from the same unbleached cotton, while an odd collection of side tables foraged from flea markets and junk shops can be unified with a couple of coats of paint.

Injections of colour also bring life and character to a room and, when used in moderation, won't over-complicate an interior. For a bold statement, paint a single wall charcoal grey and keep everything else monochrome except for one perfect pink peony, and you will have an up-to-date take on the theme. Or

ABOVE Everything in this pretty country-style kitchen is old, yet the overall feel is fresh and contemporary. A simple decorator's table and old school chairs are unified by white paint, while pink 1950s plates on the wall introduce a subtle pastel note.

OPPOSITE LEFT Dove-grey walls provide a tranquil backdrop for a selection of shapely monochrome pieces that come together to create a serene still life.

OPPOSITE ABOVE RIGHT The shadow skirting and bare white walls give this room a minimalist feel. Yet comfort has not been compromised, as the outsize armchair suggests.

OPPOSITE BELOW RIGHT Pieces of original 1960s glass bring ornate plasterwork bang up to date.

introduce colour in smaller quantities, in the shape of cushions and throws, perhaps. The key is to keep the background understated, so you do not end up with too much decorative detail.

The 'everything in moderation' rule also applies to pattern. If you have fallen in love with a bold geometric wallpaper, use it on just one wall in an otherwise plain-walled room. Add a few well-chosen streamlined retro classics, and you will successfully tone down the design while simultaneously tying it into the room scheme. Likewise, if you have found an amazing antique gilt mirror, hang it in simple surroundings so it can

take centre stage and create a focal point that adds just the right amount of drama.

How you position furniture and objects is important. A clever use of symmetry can impart a sense of serenity and harmony. For example, placing two floral-covered armchairs in a very precise arrangement beneath a window in an otherwise plain room will lessen the impact of their flowered fabric. Or you could take a cue from period interiors and create a formal seating area around a centrepiece such as a fireplace. Keep the elements casual and lively and you will avoid a stuffy 'drawing room' feel.

MAKE LIFE EASY – PLAN A
HOME THAT'S FUNCTIONAL,
WELL ORDERED AND
SMOOTH RUNNING.

function

BELOW LEFT Rich, dark tones soak up a lot of light. To combat gloom in this panelled interior, a collection of vintage mirrors has been hung in the adjacent hallway to maximize the available light. The folding double doors provide additional versatility.

BELOW CENTRE AND RIGHT Concentrating on functionality doesn't mean you have to abandon aesthetics. Coloured-glass handles make a stunning feature, while an antique silver food-dome handle has been ingeniously reused as a drawer pull.

Elegance is not only about aesthetics – it's also about precision and efficiency. To make life easy, a home should be functional, well ordered and smooth running. A well-designed interior has a calm tranquillity that stems from practicality, so at the early stages of planning an interior, it's well worth giving some thought to your lifestyle. If you take account of your routines and everyday chores when you are planning your home, time spent on mundane tasks can be halved. Jobs like unloading the dishwasher will be relatively painless if you ensure that your dinner plates are housed only an arm's length away, and the universal problem of mislaid keys can be eliminated by the simple addition of a key hook or a designated key bowl by the front door.

The layout of your living, eating and sleeping quarters also needs careful thought, so analyse how you live and then arrange your home accordingly. If you are a keen chef, it might make sense to devote a larger portion of your space to the kitchen, while a great reader could consider converting a corner of the living room into a snug library. Space dividers are a clever and versatile device and can provide visual impact as well as solving practical problems. If you have always wanted a dressing room, but have no room to spare for the purpose, one solution is to incorporate a floating wall into your bedroom to divide up the space, creating a walk-in wardrobe area behind the bed and thus leaving the sleeping area clutter-free.

Couples and those living alone might contemplate removing walls for open-plan living, but families are more likely to want to create a series of spaces that they can open up and close off to accommodate everyone's different needs. Perhaps you work from home and, despite having a designated study, always end up with your laptop open on the kitchen table. If this sounds familiar, why not incorporate a small work zone into your kitchen? Customize kitchen cabinets to provide storage for essential files, or set aside part of a sideboard to house household paperwork.

Storage is probably the most important factor when it comes to creating a functional and efficient home. Built-in cupboards/closets with sleek, flush-fitting doors are a brilliant way to hide unattractive but essential items such as washing machines, dishwashers and cleaning equipment, whereas open shelves provide practical solutions while allowing you to display favourite objects. Freestanding pieces in the shape of old wardrobes/armoires or Welsh dressers/hutches add character and originality.

Make the most of any free space you have by squeezing storage into all sorts of unlikely places. Try running a shelf along one wall of a hallway above door height to hold all your paperback

ABOVE A salvaged factory light has been rewired to create a reading lamp with a utilitarian flavour. **BELOW** This spacious open-plan apartment in an old factory building has been cleverly zoned to make several discrete areas for cooking, eating and relaxing.

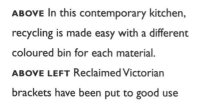

ABOVE In this contemporary kitchen, recycling is made easy with a different coloured bin for each material.
ABOVE LEFT Reclaimed Victorian brackets have been put to good use supporting broad slabs of marble to create a simple yet effective open-shelving system that showcases a collection of retro-style kitchen china in pretty pastel hues.

Both open shelves and cabinets with glazed doors can help maximize a sense of space, but you need to keep the contents tidy, as they will be constantly on show.

books; frame a doorway with cubbyholes to hold books or bottles of wine, or fix a glass shelf in front of a kitchen window to display transparent glassware yet still allow the light to filter through.

Both open shelves and cabinets with glazed doors can help maximize a sense of space, but you will need to keep the contents tidy as they will be constantly on show. Custom-built units are another great space-saver – they take up less room and hold more. Blend them into your surroundings by incorporating them into a panelled wall, or install a run of white lacquered

doors that make a simple, modern statement but do double duty by bouncing light back into a room. Alternatively, if you want a more personal feel, seek out salvaged doors in antique shops or reclamation yards to add a note of warmth and individuality to your scheme.

Making the most of the available natural daylight is an important consideration. If a room is on the dark side, choose window treatments that won't obstruct the light. Wooden shutters have a puritanical practicality that is appealing, letting the light flood in when they're open and

OPPOSITE An old French dresser/hutch is roomy enough to provide a home for china, cutlery and glassware in this high-ceilinged Parisian apartment. The stripped-back finish, revealing layers of paint as well as the original wood, brings a slightly rustic feel to the otherwise sleek contemporary scheme. A clever, custom-made wine rack neatly fills a small niche in the wall beside the cupboard.

LEFT Reclaimed doors from a salvage warehouse were used to create built-in cupboards. The panelling and glazed sections bring a touch of grandeur to an otherwise spartan interior.
BELOW An old metal trunk has been given a lick of paint and a new life holding a collection of magazines. The number '6' on the front continues a numeric theme that runs through this distinctive French home.

keeping the cold out when closed. Floaty voile curtains will diffuse the light and add a softer, more feminine feel to an interior. If, on the other hand, you have a room that is flooded with brilliant sunshine at some times of the day, Venetian blinds/shades are extremely effective at controlling and directing light.

Attention to detail not only makes a huge difference to how your home functions, but also serves as a way for you to put your personal stamp on it. Even practical items can echo your decorative theme. A row of hooks hung on the wall by your dressing table is a pretty way to store jewellery; a bamboo ladder makes a charming towel rail/rod; and even the type of doorknob you choose – a sparkly multifaceted glass knob or a tactile pebble-like form – can make a style statement, as well as being a pleasure to use every day.

individuality

INSTEAD OF SLAVISHLY FOLLOWING INTERIORS TRENDS, ALLOW YOUR HOME TO REFLECT YOUR OWN INTERESTS AND EXPRESS YOUR PERSONALITY.

ABOVE A collection of handmade ceramics is displayed on a simple wooden mantelpiece.
BELOW This elegant bedroom combines antique French bedroom furniture with oriental pieces and rustic details to create an eclectic look that's truly individual.

An elegant home is one that conveys a relaxed and confident sense of self, one where the occupant's personality shines through. Not everyone wants to choose or edit their possessions in line with a particular interiors trend, and often houses that have been decorated in that way can feel strangely soulless. Easy Elegance demands that you express your personality and allow real life to add to the look rather than distract from it. Don't feel that you have to follow style stereotypes or be a slave to fashion. Your home should reflect your life.

Mixing the old with the new and the luxurious with the everyday adds contrast, injects humour and keeps the overall effect lively and personal. Holiday finds, family heirlooms and sentimental treasures should be proudly displayed, not hidden away. However, this approach needs careful consideration and a light touch if you are to avoid chaos. Express your personality, but don't go overboard – practicality and visual cohesion are essential if you are to maintain an overall effect of harmony in an interior.

If you are a serious collector or simply a great hoarder, rejoice – Easy Elegance allows for eclectic combinations. Whether you want to display your treasures en masse or create bold effects through unexpected juxtapositions, there are many ways to deal with the challenges posed by mixing mismatched items.

Keeping the background plain and simple gives furniture and accessories breathing space and allows them to speak for themselves. For instance, a selection of eighteenth-, nineteenth- and twentieth-century antiques can be unified by setting them in an ultra-modern interior.

THIS PAGE A retro Oriental poster, a vase of English garden roses and a 1970s plastic ashtray come together to create a beautiful yet quirky still-life.

OPPOSITE This wall of postcards, photos and images torn from magazines is a work of art in itself.
BELOW LEFT A chic dining area demonstrates a bold use of black, combining matt and satin surfaces to create definition. The large canvas offers light relief.

BELOW CENTRE The bicycle is part of the decor in this modern apartment. It chimes perfectly with the utilitarian feel of the chair and tallboy-style unit.
BELOW RIGHT A staircase and hallway have been painted with a clever *trompe l'oeil* carpet effect.

A collection of scatter cushions made from vintage silk headscarves could look slightly overpowering, but when placed on a minimalist white sofa they are, in a sense, 'framed' – the sofa acts as a backdrop against which to display them.

Colour is also a powerful instrument. By using different shades of a single colour family, you can blend different styles so they hang together harmoniously. A calming combination of greys, beiges, browns and whites, for example, can tie together a mismatched set of bedroom furniture. Start with buff-coloured walls, add a French carved wooden bed painted pearl grey and upholstered in pewter-coloured satin damask,

then add a rustic cupboard painted taupe, all set upon a roughly finished wood floor.

To dress the room, throw in a pair of 1970s white plastic bedside tables and finish with two 1920s smoky-grey cut-glass bedside lamps. The muted palette will unify these disparate elements to create a unique room scheme.

Collections play a large part in personalizing your home, and how you choose to display them is significant. Whatever your obsession – antique hunting trophies, old typesetters' numbers and letters, vintage ceramics or even retro Barbie dolls – they can all be used to make your mark. If you avidly collect vintage china, don't confine it

ABOVE Reclaimed antique French shutters have been given a new lease of life as cupboard/closet doors. Picture frames are charmingly and conveniently hung on the wall and makeshift tables have been fashioned from sawn logs and green sticks. A small woodburning stove keeps the cabin warm in the winter, while vintage cushions add colour and a hint of femininity.

RIGHT A Victorian print, a pair of antique shears and a coloured-glass candleholder are artlessly arranged on a shelf made from old scaffolding planks and supported on rusted Victorian brackets. **FAR RIGHT** Pieces of salvaged plasterwork and a ball of string make an informal but decorative display on a windowsill.

to a dresser/hutch – instead, cover a wall in old plates of varying designs for a stunning decorative statement. Holiday finds such as pebbles and shells look beautiful lined up on windowsills or in bowls, and you can also show off kitsch souvenirs like snow globes or a model of the Eiffel Tower. Displayed beside more restrained items, they add a whimsical note that is both refreshing and lively.

Another way of ensuring that your home is a true reflection of yourself is to commission one-off pieces or customize existing ones. Reclamation businesses and builders' yards are excellent sources of inspiration. Old railway sleepers/railroad ties, sliced lengthways into planks, would make a good tabletop. For a genuinely original dining table, combine them with a galvanized scaffolding pole base. Other architectural salvage worth keeping an eye open for includes old water-tank brackets, which look great when used to support chunky shelves or an overmantel, shutters that can be transformed into a bedhead, or an old industrial winch, which could be given a new lease of life as a homemade rise-and-fall pendant light.

Whatever your obsession – antique hunting trophies, old typesetters' letters, vintage ceramics, or even retro Barbie dolls – they can all be used to make your mark.

LEFT Old French cheese moulds have been hung on the wall and reinvented as box shelves to showcase a collection of antique teacups. In the background, a 1960s sequinned top in a box frame creates a striking and personal work of art.
RIGHT Shells, starfish, pieces of coral and other beach finds from around the world are displayed in a glass cabinet and act as a constant reminder of past holidays.

Setting the scene

Easy Elegance isn't about following strict design rules or rigorous style blueprints. Instead, it's about a chic, relaxed way of living and a home that suits your tastes and lifestyle. Based on five flexible interior themes, this section will help you find the Easy Elegance look that suits you best, so your home can reflect your personality.

modern elegance

THIS FACET OF THE EASY ELEGANCE LOOK
PLAYS AROUND WITH CLASSICAL AND
CONTEMPORARY ELEMENTS AND TEAMS
THEM IN UNEXPECTED WAYS.

Nowadays, what does 'modern' mean to us? The *Compact Oxford English Dictionary* defines it as 'relating to present or to recent times … characterized by or using the most up-to-date techniques or equipment.' Such a definition may conjure up images of sleek, high-tech interiors with glass walls, steel doors and injection-moulded plastic furniture, but with the growing dominance of a few powerful retail brands and with people becoming concerned about excessive consumerism and their carbon footprints, the word modern has come to mean much more. Ecological awareness, a renewed appreciation of individuality, and a reaction against global retail monopolies has spawned a softer, more gentle form of modernism. Mixing the

Mixing the old with the new, looking for furniture with green credentials and using high-tech energy-saving devices, along with a desire to be different – these strands have come together to create Modern Elegance.

old with the new, looking for furniture with green credentials and using high-tech energy-saving devices, along with a desire to be different – these different strands have come together to create Modern Elegance – a look that mixes the streamlined and modern with the unexpected and understated.

OPPOSITE A well-worn Eames Lounge Chair and Saarinen's Tulip side table are the epitome of Easy Elegance in this minimalist country interior. The blowsy white hydrangea adds an unexpected touch of femininity.

THIS PAGE, TOP TO BOTTOM Natural materials add a sensual touch to a modern interior; white china on a black shelf looks clean and simple; ceramic nightlights resembling sea urchins are a pretty detail in a modern bathroom.

Modern Elegance takes a playful approach to interior design, combining classical and contemporary elements in contradictory ways. This might mean incorporating eighteenth-century antiques into a slick, eco-friendly new home to soften what might otherwise be a somewhat clinical space. Other ideas include old-fashioned buttoning on an ultra-sleek sofa for a hint of Savile Row traditionalism, or transforming a second-hand pine table with black paint and the addition of industrial-sized castors to create a chic modern one-off design.

Whether you live in an architect-designed converted barn or a tiny townhouse, don't feel you have to obey clichéd style rules. Modern Elegance is about decorative fusion – combining hard and soft, natural and manmade, quirky and traditional – and this ethos applies to the walls as much as any other factor in the room.

In a very minimal interior, wall decoration can be used to contribute texture and interest. Soften exposed brick walls by painting them warm shades of dove grey or dusky pink. Cover a chimney breast in metallic mosaic tiles to cast a warm glow, or line an entire wall with stacked logs. Conversely, you may live in a period house that abounds in original features. If this is the case, keep the background simple. If you have

RIGHT The combination of traditional panelling and modern accessories creates a cosy feel that is slick and contemporary.

OPPOSITE LEFT The owners of this converted electrical factory have managed to create a soft modernity by juxtaposing different styles and genres. The industrial architecture of the building makes a stunning backdrop to the 1970s sofa, while the crystal chandelier and Gustavian-style chest of drawers add glamour.

OPPOSITE RIGHT Painted a matt slate grey and upholstered in white and charcoal linen, this French Bergère chair takes on a contemporary feel.

OPPOSITE This elegant hallway in an Edwardian townhouse boasts all its original decorative features, yet the addition of a ceramic-tiled floor and contemporary pieces makes it feel distinctly clean and modern. **RIGHT** Despite the solid, pared-down shapes of the table and bench and the cool all-white colour scheme, this dining area is saved from severity by the splashes of pink and the crystal chandelier, which combine to create a look that's fresh and pretty.

panelling, paint it all the same colour, or strip it for a distressed, peeling effect, and contrast this with slick, clean-lined contemporary furniture.

Approach flooring and window treatments in the same way, counterbalancing different materials and styles. Bare floorboards create a sense of monastic simplicity that makes a good background for anything glossy and new. In an old house, reverse the scheme, using a slick ceramic-tiled floor to bring glamour to a period townhouse. Shutters or blinds/shades are ideal if

you want an unobtrusive backdrop, but for an opulent effect consider statement curtains, such as a pair of full-length, ice-blue Gaufrage velvet drapes in an all-white room. If privacy is an issue, sheer curtains are a good solution. But rather than confining sheers to the width of the window alone, try running them the entire length of the window wall along a concealed track for a more dramatic, fuss-free look. Alternatively, hang a huge oversized pendant drum lightshade in front of the window to block the view from outside.

LEFT AND BELOW A long kitchen workbench makes a stunning statement in this sleek apartment. Open shelves keep the look relaxed, while the pale aqua paint adds soft colour. On the wall behind, photos hung from bulldog clips add interest.

Colour can be used to add contrast and surprise. Give heritage hues an exciting twist by teaming them with flashes of vibrant neon, or be bold and use black as a neutral background colour. Treat the black as you would white, layering different shades such as charcoal, slate and battleship grey with varying textures – gloss paint, matt felt, and the sheen of ponyskin – to add depth and interest. Ice-cream pastels, on the other hand, introduce a note of femininity into a stark masculine interior.

When it comes to furniture, this look is all about how you treat and where you place the items you have, rather than requiring design classics or trophy pieces. An antique highbacked sofa will take on an funky avant-garde air when covered in tangerine cotton, just as a set of Philippe Starck's perspex Ghost chairs will update an oak dining table. Salvaged ex-industrial furniture has a no-nonsense honesty that adds utilitarian chic to any scheme, as does professional catering equipment in the kitchen.

How you tackle accessories will depend on your chosen look. If you have opted for minimalism, a few carefully selected items will be enough to provide interest. If, however, you are an avid collector and your taste verges on the maximalist, then showcase your treasures with humour, ingenuity and wit. The result should be funky, not fuddy-duddy.

THIS PAGE A table once used for sorting potatoes has been combined with a set of antique chairs in a warehouse apartment in Amsterdam. Although most of the elements are old, the sheer simplicity of the layout creates a look that feels modern in spirit.

country elegance

PUT A CONTEMPORARY
SPIN ON COUNTRY
STYLE TO CREATE A
HOME THAT COMBINES
UTILITARIAN CHIC
WITH RUSTIC CHARM.

It doesn't matter whether you live in a small village or in the heart of the city, country style has an enduring appeal. Well-crafted pieces made from natural materials such as wood, stone, cotton, linen and wool are the mainstays of this look – materials that will stand the test of time, whether they are brand-new or second-hand.

There are several angles from which you can approach the country look – manor house, country cottage, rustic cabin or modern barn. Whichever you choose, Country Elegance allows you to reinterpret the traditional elements of rustic style and strip away frills and clutter. The result is a fresher, pared-down country look with its roots in utility rather than romance.

Country Elegance allows you to reinterpret the traditional elements of rustic style and strip away frills and clutter. The result is a fresher, pared-down country look with its roots in utility rather than romance.

Tongue-and-groove, wooden panelling or rough limewashed plaster finishes give walls an authentic country feel, but there are other alternatives. In a small, low-ceiling cottage, an oversized, flamboyantly patterned wallpaper will add an unexpected twist of grandeur, while bare concrete walls and sliding glass doors, normally associated with minimalist

THIS PAGE AND OPPOSITE
A French carved sofa adds a note of elegance to this rustic cabin, but it has been left uncovered in keeping with the simplicity of the interior. Reclaimed scaffolding boards have been used on the floor, while the walls are clad with white-painted planking. Vintage floral cotton cushions add some colour and ornate sari edgings are displayed in a bowl along with natural objects found on long country walks.

LEFT A pair of cosy white armchairs create an inviting seating area in this bedroom. The unbleached linen curtains diffuse the light. **BELOW** Farrow & Ball wallpaper creates a bold backdrop for a bed made from old banister ends and reclaimed wood.

interiors, can offer a contrasting yet sympathetic backdrop to a living room furnished with simple handcrafted pieces. The floor, like the walls, should have a slightly rugged feel – chunky, bleached floorboards, slate tiles, broad flagstones and worn brick all have a straightforward integrity that is perfect for country elegance.

A country home isn't complete without a fireplace or wood-burning stove. Look out for reclaimed stone slabs to use as a hearth, or old beams to set into the wall over a fireplace aperture. Salvage yards are great places to pick up old grates and mantelpieces.

Colours should take their cue from nature. Be inspired by the changing seasons. A winter beachscape provides a cool palette of greys, blues and beiges, while a spring morning might suggest earthy browns, acid greens and splashes of pink. If you look carefully, you will be amazed at how bold nature's colour combinations can be.

Window treatments should be simple and unassuming. Antique linen sheets make instant curtains, while old tablecloths can be used as café curtains. Drapes made from linen scrim bring a down-to-earth feel, while pretty floral chintzes have a vintage flavour. Shutters will lend a country cottage a touch of grandeur.

When it comes to furniture and accessories, mixing up old and new will prevent your home from looking like a set from a costume drama.

THIS PAGE The charm of this magnificent light-flooded hallway in a Georgian country house lies in the contrast between the sweeping manorial staircase and the timeworn flagstones and humble brick floor. A collection of antique apothecary jars sits on the hall table, along with a pretty 1920s lamp with pale blue silk shades and a pair of old wooden shoe lasts.

A big, squashy sofa and armchairs in hardwearing fabrics like denim, canvas or mattress ticking, teamed with a modern footstool, vintage cushions and a sleek modern aluminium floor lamp, will create a utilitarian country look that's both practical and comfortable.

Good storage is essential. Old wooden trunks hold large quantities and can double as coffee tables, while stacking baskets by the front door can house shoes, hats and gloves. Wall-mounted plate racks lend a air of quaintness, but if you are after a more hard-edged look, Shaker-style cabinets inject a note of elegant austerity.

When it comes to the finishing touches, nothing beats the beauty of nature, so bring the outside in: branches of blossom in spring, roses in summer, wide bowls of conkers and seedpods in the autumn, and armfuls of twigs or abandoned birds' nests in winter.

OPPOSITE LEFT Tongue-and-groove walls and pale grey accessories give this pretty bathroom a Scandinavian feel.

OPPOSITE RIGHT By painting everything white, the owners of this sunny dining room have created a country look that feels fresh and contemporary.

OPPOSITE BELOW Despite its lofty proportions and original panelling, the simple floor treatment and spare furnishings make this rather grand Georgian interior feel relaxed and informal.

RIGHT A monochrome palette and simple lines lend this kitchen a contemporary feel, despite its many references to the past.

BELOW RIGHT An original brick floor, wooden worktops and a butler's sink combine to create the quintessential country kitchen.

BELOW LEFT Antique country chairs, rough brick floors, original panelled walls and an inglenook fireplace come together to create a tranquil dining room.

retro elegance

PAY HOMAGE TO RETRO STYLE BY COMBINING VINTAGE PIECES AND DESIGN CLASSICS WITH CAREFULLY CHOSEN MODERN ITEMS TO CREATE AN EASY AND ELEGANT INTERIOR.

Retro Elegance looks beyond the obvious references – 1950s mid-century modernism and 1960s pop culture – to discover a more sophisticated retro style with an elegant twist. Discard any notions you may have about collecting design icons, vintage memorabilia or trophy pieces, and instead focus on sourcing and enjoying items from the recent past, respecting time-honoured classics and using them for the purpose for which they were originally intended.

While the Retro Elegance approach allows for keen collecting, resist the urge to surround yourself with antiquated relics – you don't want to live in a museum. Getting the look right calls for a measure of

The important thing is to keep the background clean and simple, so that the overall effect is coolly modern rather than cluttered or fusty. This will allow you successfully to mix pieces from different eras.

restraint and a degree of self-confidence. The important thing is to keep the background clean and simple, so that the overall effect is coolly modern, not cluttered or fusty. This will allow you successfully to mix pieces from different eras and place them in unexpected settings. A classic Eames' Lounge Chair, for instance, would bring an injection of cool to a country cottage,

OPPOSITE A streamlined sideboard is adorned with modern and ethnic items for a modern take on the retro theme. **ABOVE LEFT** A collection of 1950s red spotted china adds a vibrant shot of colour to an all-white kitchen.

ABOVE RIGHT A vintage soft-drinks crate has been ingeniously reused as a home for cookery books perched on top of a curvy, mint-green 1950s-inspired fridge. **LEFT** These velvety dahlias have a fabulous retro charm.

LEFT Organically shaped mid-century glassware adds colour and sensual form to a traditional panelled room and clashes beautifully with the hot-pink orchid.

BELOW A retro-inspired dress by Celia Birtwell hangs in front of vintage wallpaper in an elegant Georgian house that hasn't been redecorated since the 1950s.

OPPOSITE In the corner of this room, an eclectic combination of style, colour and pattern creates a rich still-life. A 1950s fabric screen is teamed with Cole & Son wallpaper and a contemporary black, cast-resin console table, while pieces of post-war glassware add vivid splashes of colour that bring the scene to life.

while an original Robin Day Club Sofa would add a note of tailored formality to a living room papered in quirky vintage wallpaper.

Creating this look isn't just about collecting design classics and vintage pieces. The actual bones of your home needs careful consideration if you are to get the right balance between modern-day living and retro homage. If subtlety is what you seek, keep walls and floors simple and unassuming. Plain paint will create a clean background while grounding the look in the twenty-first century. Choose the ubiquitous pure white for a cool, clean art-gallery feel, or opt for deeper, sensual tones like dark olive or purple-brown for an intimate, sexy look.

If a full-on retro theme is what you're aiming for, consider 1970s-style dark wood panelling, laminate kitchen splashbacks in 1950s-inspired candy colours, or a stone-clad chimney breast that's reminiscent of 1960s kitsch. Vintage wallpapers and tiles are a great way to introduce pattern, but as these are not always available in the quantities required, you may prefer to

OPPOSITE These 1960s chairs have cushions covered with fabrics of the same vintage and are teamed with a contemporary table in this peaceful dining room.

ABOVE LEFT A 1970s Danish leather sofa, a 1960s sideboard and modern accessories create a retro look that's fresh and modern.
ABOVE RIGHT Sleek black floors provide a striking backdrop for this 1950s chair.

investigate modern-day retro-inspired styles. Try subway tiles in pale aqua in an Art Deco-style bathroom; or opt for bold geometric flower designs for a touch of 1960s suburbia. For a subtler approach, choose contemporary styles in retro hues such as chocolate or avocado, to give a hint of the 1970s home.

Retro style is well represented in the furniture world, and many designs by iconic twentieth-century style pioneers such as Marcel Breuer, Mies Van de Rohe, and Eileen Gray look as if they were designed just yesterday. Many are still in production, and look every bit as 'modern' as much of the contemporary design emerging from today's studios. But there is an irreplaceable charm about original pieces, because they reveal their history through their wear and tear, outdated manufacturing techniques and original colours.

If your budget allows, buying original design classics is a great investment, but it is by no means essential for the Retro Elegance look. The twentieth century witnessed the birth of mass production and many products, especially those by prolific companies such as Ercol, Kartell, or even good old Woolworths, are easily uncovered. Junk shops, flea markets, charity shops/thrift stores and Ebay are all great sources of affordable vintage finds.

The golden rule with retro ingredients is that if you like something, you should embrace and incorporate it. That said, try not to get stuck in a timewarp, and remember that an eclectic, magpie instinct is always to be encouraged. Keep your scheme fresh and lively by adding modern accessories, ethnic crafted pieces or even some traditional antiques.

feminine elegance

THOSE WHO SEEK THE FEMININITY OF PRETTINESS, SOFT EDGES, PASTEL COLOURS AND CURVACEOUS LINES NEED LOOK NO FURTHER.

If you crave prettiness, sugared-almond shades and soft edges, then Feminine Elegance is guaranteed to appeal. Crystal chandeliers, floral fabrics, wallpaper and carved French beds are the building blocks of this sensual, romantic and unashamedly pretty look.

There are so many different strands to the feminine look – delicate chinoiserie, Art Deco glamour and French-inspired shabby chic, to name but a few – and you might consider decorating an entire room using just one of these styles. But to make your interior entirely individual, combine two or more strands, or just pick out

Femininity and theatricality are key to this look. Indulge in glamorous decorative touches, but add contrasting details to bring a sharper edge and prevent your space from becoming too frilly and fussy.

one or two ideas to add a dash of femininity, then allow them breathing space using contrast.

Feminine prettiness is, of course, inherently girly, but in the Easy Elegance home an element of restraint always comes into play. Counterbalance the feminine charms of chintzy floral wallpaper by combining it with bare, whitewashed

OPPOSITE The frivolous prettiness of this wallpaper is tempered by the rough floorboards, while splashes of black in the form of a vintage eiderdown and a mother-of-pearl inlaid chair help to ground the colour.

THIS PAGE, TOP TO BOTTOM Vintage costume jewellery adorns a mantelpiece; a crystal chandelier adds sparkle and glamour to a room; an ornate vintage lamp works well against white walls, while the starfish adds a personal touch.

LEFT A pretty metalwork sofa strewn with vintage floral cushions adds decorative detail to the corner of this simple bedroom. A antique child's dress hangs on the wardrobe doorframe, and a dazzling fuchsia-pink silk curtain adds some theatrical drama while also lending the room a warm glow.

OPPOSITE LEFT The vibrant shades of aqua, pink and orange on this beautiful cushion made from old kimono fabric shine out against a neutral-coloured chaise in an all-white room.

OPPOSITE RIGHT A modern take on an eighteenth-century chinoiserie theme: decorative shoe boxes with an exotic flavour and a pair of oriental slippers sit happily beside a delicately carved chair, which is all the more charming for being a little scuffed and battered.

floorboards, for example, or toss an unexpected element into the mix by positioning a battered, even shabby, Louis XVI chair in front of a wall covered with orientally inspired, cherry-blossom-patterned wallpaper. It is these unexpected contrasts that bring a sense of informality, spontaneity and ease to a room and prevent it from becoming too saccharine or a period pastiche. The key is not to overdo the feminine angle – less is definitely more.

Start with the bare bones of the room – the walls, floor and windows. Keep the space deliberately understated in order to create a clean backdrop for your carefully selected feminine flourishes. Untreated or painted wooden boards are usually the best choice for flooring, as they possess a simplicity that tones down any tendencies towards over-elaboration.

You can paint, stain or wash your floorboards, depending on your taste and your scheme.

With this look, it pays to be adventurous with colour – while summery pastels are sure to create a pretty, ladylike feel, bolder colours like hot pinks, acid greens and bright turquoise can lift a scheme, whether it be light or dark, and provide deeper colour accents that will give an interior a sharper modern edge.

If your walls are panelled, consider painting them all one colour to simplify the scheme. If you want to pick out attractive architectural details, do so in a subtle way, choosing a colour that's one shade darker or lighter than your main one. Alternatively, add pattern with ornate wallpaper, or inject some Hollywood glamour in the form of fabric panels. A padded silk-damask wall would make a stunning centrepiece in a living room, as

ABOVE This elegant dining room is a clever mix of contemporary simplicity and decorative femininity. A glass-fronted armoire, painted palest pink, sits against chalky grey walls, while sleek white leather chairs add a sharp edge.

long as you keep the rest of the elements simple, while a classic toile de Jouy calico in faded tones will give a French boudoir twist to a bedroom.

Window treatments should either complement or contrast with the walls. If you have opted for a plain, minimalist finish on the walls, then take the opportunity to play around and have some fun with the window treatments. Perhaps experiment with an antique-lace panel dyed indigo for a touch of theatrical drama, or trawl Ebay for a pair of vintage-linen curtains in a floral print.

When it comes to furniture, mix up contemporary and traditional pieces. Juxtaposing differing styles keeps a scheme loose and prevents it from becoming clichéd. A pretty glazed French armoire, painted a chalky pink or grey, will make a gorgeous focal point in a dining room, but contrast it with a sleek modern dining table and chairs to stop the room looking like a stage set.

In the living room, it's best to temper femininity with practicality, as this room has to stand up to the wear and tear of day-to-day living. A shapely scroll-armed sofa will lend any room a feminine feel, while the curvaceous lines of a chaise longue are indisputably sexy. If you like a clean tailored look and have chosen furnishings that are sleek and formal, soften any hard edges by adding sequinned cushions, deep rugs and tactile mohair throws. By the same token, an ultra-modern apartment can be given a splash of contemporary prettiness with the addition of a few carefully selected feminine touches, such as upholstery fabrics in chalky pastel hues, ornate Venetian glass mirrors and a decorative floral needlepoint rug.

Alternatively, if it's an air of bohemian chic that you're hoping to achieve, adopt a more eclectic approach, dressing your room with antique or modern crystal chandeliers, a spangly Moroccan

OPPOSITE ABOVE AND BELOW RIGHT A delicate vintage teacup sits alongside a curvy modern jug; simple modern vases give the decorative details more impact in this pretty room and keep the scheme on the right side of sentimentality.

ABOVE This glamorous boudoir oozes femininity and sensuality. An Italian gilt sofa is piled with cushions made from fabric remnants. The neutral shades of the padded wall, panelling and floor tone down the decorative details.

BELOW Vintage moiré striped wallpaper verges on the kitsch, but the pink polka-dot fabric gives this antique French bed a fresh, pretty feel and saves the room from feeling grungy.

RIGHT AND OPPOSITE Delicate colours create a feminine effect in this bedroom. A sequinned top makes a striking artwork, and the box shelves are old French cheese moulds.

bedspread tossed over the sofa; a pair of vintage 1950s side lamps and pieces of Murano glass in richly seductive shades of deep rose, chartreuse or turquoise.

Bedrooms and bathrooms are the ideal place to demonstrate feminine decorating skills, as they lend themselves perfectly to a romantic scheme. Today's vast choice of beds might includes a four-poster draped in richly coloured saris; a Victorian cast-iron bedstead heaped with pretty embroidered bed linen; and a carved wood bateau lit piled with vintage eiderdowns – all of these will impart just the right amount of romance and seductive glamour. Don't dismiss their modern counterparts, either. A sleek stainless-steel bed frame can be given the feminine treatment by setting it against pastel-painted walls and dressing it up with contemporary floral bed linen. In the bathroom think of rolltop bathtubs, traditional Edwardian basins and decorative glass jars filled with an array of lotions and potions for a girly sanctuary.

faded elegance

EMBRACE FADED BEAUTY, ARTFUL NEGLECT AND
STYLISH DILAPIDATION WITH THIS NOSTALGIC,
ECLECTIC SPIN ON EASY ELEGANCE.

Faded Elegance demonstrates that grandeur doesn't have to equal ostentation. An appreciation of the imperfect and an eclectic eye lie at its heart, and faded wallpaper, well-worn floors and fraying fabrics are treasured for their patina of age and the timeless ambience that they bestow. Pristine new pieces are shunned in favour of chipped gilt and an air of artful neglect in order to create a look that is edgy rather than dowdy, but elegant nonetheless.

However, modern elements are essential if you want to prevent your home becoming a monument to nostalgia. Adding a judicious selection of clean-lined contemporary pieces will

A far cry from glossy showhomes with their perfect paintwork and plush flooring, this look celebrates the old, the chipped, the scuffed and the imperfect, relishing their beautiful patina of age and timeless appeal.

prevent an interior from looking too formal or fussy and will keep your home firmly rooted in the twenty-first century. For example, in a slick minimalist interior, a worn, slightly battered Bergère chair will be imbued with a more casual up-to-date appeal, while a clean-lined modern chair

OPPOSITE The man who sold this elegant antique bench to its current owners offered to recommend a caner who could repair the damaged seat, but their reply was that, for them, its shabbiness was the secret of its appeal.

THIS PAGE, TOP TO BOTTOM A ceramic rose is in good company with a pile of dusty old books; original paintwork in a house that hasn't been redecorated in 50 years has a soft faded patina; a silk rose adorns a vintage chandelier.

BELOW LEFT A rusty metal table looks perfectly at home on the old brick floor of this country farmhouse.
BELOW MIDDLE The shredded seat cover and faded paint on this antique French carved sofa only add to its allure, giving it character and interest.

BELOW RIGHT An antique crystal chandelier has been casually hung at the window, where it can catch some natural daylight and help reflect it back into the room. A delicate lace-trimmed hand towel has been put into service as a curtain panel.

placed in front of a crumbling plaster wall will instantly transform the mood from dreary decay to stylish dilapidation.

Dusky tones, sepia tints and worn textures are all key to this look. The fleshy pinks and antique whites of bare plaster have a dusty, chalky finish that imparts exactly the right feel to walls, but if replastering is not an option you can recreate this look with a paint finish instead or, alternatively, strip the walls back to reveal layers of old wallpaper or paintwork that can resemble works of art in themselves.

You may be fortunate enough to have original panelling in your home, but if not consider adding some to bring definition to the walls. Remember that the proportions of the panelling must suit

the style of the room. A Georgian house, for instance, will need a simple, classic design of square dimensions, while an Edwardian interior will allow for panels that are taller and more ornate, and a cottage will call for tongue-and-groove panelling. However, there is nothing to say that you can't play around with proportions and styles, fitting a section of grand oak panelling into a small, modest room. Salvage yards are always great sources of antique panelling.

When it comes to floors, the more battered the better for this particular look. Pull up your carpets to expose the original floorboards underneath. Don't be put off if they are in bad condition – it will only add to the character of the room. Rotten boards should be cut out and

RIGHT What looks like a simple arrangement is actually a carefully considered collection of textures and surfaces that give this calm, tranquil room a serene beauty. The chalky plaster walls and the bare boards are a perfect backdrop for an old tailor's dummy dressed with strings of beads, a postal basket and a straw shopping bag. The ornate gilt mirror and crystal chandelier add touches of glamour.

THIS PAGE An elegant panelled room takes on a modern club feel with the introduction of a slick contemporary chair and a 1970s marble-topped side table. The bright orange cushion provides a vivid splash of colour.

RIGHT In a cloakroom, plaster walls have been hand-painted to look like a faded fresco.
BELOW Rough plaster, bare boards, sensuous velvet, crumpled linen and a pair of antlers provide a variety of textures that transform a potentially austere bedroom into a soothing haven.

replaced with reclaimed ones, while small holes can be repaired by nailing tin panels over them, or by cutting in small sections of new wood and staining it to match the original. Repairs or additions of this kind will enhance the floor's patina of age, as well as enabling it to soldier on for another generation. Floor finishes should be as simple as possible. You may love your bare boards as they are, or, if you prefer a cleaner, more polished look, sand them back and give them a coat of wax or matt varnish for a deep, warm tone. For a lighter, Scandinavian feel, bleach boards with lye then seal them with an application of Danish white soap.

When it comes to furniture, the good news is that you are often able to snap up bargains in the form of less-than-perfect pieces that have been rejected by more serious collectors. These might include a Regency wing-backed armchair with the stuffing slightly exposed; a nineteenth-century rococo bed with threadbare satin upholstery; a rusting Parisian café table; or a Gustavian console table with scuffed paintwork. All have their own particular faded charm. However, your choice of furniture will depend on whether you intend to devote your entire decorating scheme to past times, whether you want to select just a few antique pieces to add interest to a modern interior, or just to sharpen up a faded interior with the addition of one or two sleek modern

LEFT AND OPPOSITE
A salvaged door bearing layers of paint and scraps of old wallpaper has become an art installation. An antique monogrammed linen sheet is thrown over the contemporary box-shaped armchair. while an upturned fruit crate acts as a side table. The green glass jar holds peonies and stocks in pinks and reds that echo the colours in the wallpaper behind.

pieces, like a tailored Cappellini sofa or a modern antique such as Hans Wegner's sleek, curvaceous mid-century Wishbone Chair.

As always, accessories offer the opportunity to have fun and add elements of contrast. While crystal wall sconces, twinkling chandeliers and remnants of decorative plaster mouldings will happily complete the Faded Elegance look, elements of the unexpected will also keep the

scheme feeling vibrant and modern. A gold-threaded sari draped across a battered leather armchair and teamed with a pretty floral cushion adds a glamorous twist, contemporary hand-crafted ceramics and glass bring a modern aesthetic and the raw textures of hand-knitted throws, antique linen and natural finds, such as pieces of coral, roughly hewn logs or even fresh flowers, will all add a sensual earthy element.

elegant *living*

Now you have an understanding of the main
principles of Easy Elegance, you can set about
the task of designing specific rooms. This section
takes you through each area of the home, offering
practical tips and style suggestions that will help
you put your ideas into practice. The result will
be a home that is stylish, beautiful and, most
important of all, a great place to live.

living rooms

TODAY'S LIVING ROOM MUST BE PRACTICAL AND VERSATILE, BOTH A PRIVATE SANCTUARY AND A SOCIABLE SPACE FOR ENTERTAINING.

ABOVE Sage-green walls and original parquet flooring provide a coolly classic background for a collection of contemporary pieces and treasured family heirlooms. A sofa covered in neutral-coloured linen is softened by the addition of a collection of chintzy floral cushions in pink and blue accent colours. Both the colour and the style of the cushions echo the casual arrangement of garden flowers, the handpainted design on the pretty antique lamp base and the retro fringed lampshade.

A far cry from the formal drawing room of the past and the over-the-top yet curiously sterile interior-designed show home, the Easy Elegance living room reflects its occupants' personalities and lifestyles. It's a relaxed and comforting space, somewhere to unwind surrounded by the objects that you treasure.

The living room is one of the most hard-working rooms in the home. Busy modern lifestyles demand that it accommodates a multitude of different activities – entertaining, reading, watching television, listening to music or simply sitting and daydreaming – so practicality and versatility are essential. Usually the first port of call for visitors, it is a public forum, a place where you make your mark in terms of taste and identity, as everything you display tells a story about your life. Books, music, family photos, memorabilia – all reveal something about your history and personality.

The first consideration is how and by whom your living room will be used. Some families may want to opt for two or three small interconnecting rooms, while others might prefer to blur the traditional boundaries with a free-flowing arrangement reminiscent of a loft apartment. Room dividers are a particularly effective way to increase the flexibility of your space. If you have knocked two rooms together, consider installing sliding or folding doors

THIS PAGE This inviting sitting room combines a clever mix of traditional, vintage, global and contemporary styles that all work together to create a very personal yet entirely cohesive scheme. The squashy pink sofa shouts comfort, luxury and relaxed living all at once. The simple fireplace treatment adds a minimal modern slant, while an African leather footstool brings a dash of eclectic cool.

OPPOSITE AND BELOW This decor in this
room has not been changed for decades, but
the modern sofa and 1920s mirrored table
bring it up to date in a quirky, original way.
RIGHT Vintage glassware stands out against the
richly coloured walls.

between them to allow you to close off one area
when privacy is needed or to open them up
when one big space is called for.

Alternatively, you may prefer to use large
pieces of furniture or freestanding shelving units
to create different zones within a single space.
Placed in the middle of a room and opposite
a focal point such as a fireplace, a high-backed
Knole sofa will create a cosy seating area that
feels intimate and secluded, while substantial
pieces of storage, such as bookcases, can be
placed at right angles to an exterior wall to
section off a quiet reading area. Choose a sleek,
see-through modern shelving system by a
manufacturer like Vitsoe for a light contemporary
feel, or seek out old shop or museum display
cabinets in salvage yards for a more eclectic look.

Another way to divide a space is by using
a variety of wall treatments. Finish walls in
traditional lime plaster for a cosy cottage feel,
then create a secluded library corner by cladding
part of the walls in tongue-and-groove panelling.
Music lovers could create a dedicated music
area with hessian walls for a funky 1970s vibe
(fabric-covered walls have the added benefit of
improving acoustics). Or define a lounging zone
with a retro-inspired wallpaper. Those who tend
towards minimalism can use different finishes –
concrete, glass or gloss paint – to differentiate
between areas for eating, relaxing or socializing.

LEFT A cushion made from an old lace blouse found in a charity shop is the perfect addition to this opulent, feminine living room.

BELOW The soft chalky colours and earthy textures of this serene living room help to tie together traditional and ethnic elements to create a cosy, inviting interior. A huge mirror, casually propped against the wall, reflects more light into the room and a shell chandelier adds delicate detail. The painting is by Peter Ellison.

OPPOSITE A huge bay window allows natural daylight to flood into this informal, understated living room in an elegant seaside townhouse. Cushions made from vintage silk scarves introduce colour and pattern into an otherwise neutral interior. The white animal-skin rug adds warmth to the painted floorboards, while darker accents help to ground the colour scheme. A single reclaimed shutter makes an interesting ornament in the corner.

Flooring, on the other hand, needs to be uniform throughout to maximize the sense of space. Reception rooms generally have high traffic, so choose something that is hardwearing and will only improve with wear and tear. Wooden floorboards are always warm and welcoming. Natural oak will develop a beautiful silvery tone over time. If you are laying pine flooring, you can prevent it from turning orange by applying lye then Danish white soap. There are also specialist companies that produce floor paint designed for floorboards or even concrete, and some of them will mix paint especially to match your colour scheme.

The perfect living room has some sort of fireplace or woodburning stove. Few people can resist the opportunity to bask in the warmth of

OPPOSITE An antique Bergère chair has been given the Easy Elegance treatment and stripped back to its hessian underclothes. The silk damask cushion hints at its original covering.

RIGHT A huge blown-up print from a fashion advertising campaign dominates this living space in a converted factory. The current owners have successfully brought together a deconstructed 1970s sofa, a French country cabinet and a Gustavian chest of drawers by using a soft colour scheme of whites, greys and greens.

a real log fire – it will inevitably become a focal point. Many period homes still have a chimneybreast with an original surround, but if yours has been removed, it's easy to reinstate. Reclamation yards are the best place to search for replacements, but if you are after a cleaner, more contemporary look, then a simple, unadorned aperture is a great alternative.

When it comes to furniture, your single most important investment is the sofa. Comfort is the primary concern, so choose the best and biggest model that you can afford and have room for. If you are buying a new sofa, whether it be modern or traditional in style, it has to be long-lasting, so go for something with classic lines that won't date. Even if your budget is small, try to

BELOW LEFT, CENTRE AND RIGHT A bubblegum-pink ottoman offers a bold splash of colour in this neutral scheme. The clean lines of the seating system are softened with floral cushions. The drawing above the sofa is by the Australian artist Brett Whitely.

OPPOSITE Deep, squashy armchairs, layers of tactile fabrics and varying shades of white and warm neutrals prove that pale colour schemes don't have to feel cold and clinical. The cosy window seat provides an inviting spot for an afternoon nap.

avoid mass-produced high-street pieces – however alluring their prices might seem, they are rarely very comfortable or durable. Instead, hunt for sofas in house clearance sales, auctions, second-hand shops or antique centres, where a little diligent searching will turn up good-quality, handmade models that were built to last yet won't break the bank. Don't be put off by drab upholstery or tatty covers – as long as a sofa is comfortable, you can transform it with new upholstery, loose covers/slipcovers or throws.

For a casual country scheme, choose tactile upholstery fabrics such as corduroy or linen sacking in natural or neutral shades. If you are seeking a touch of elegant femininity, look for vintage-style florals or smooth linen in dusky pastel. For a clean, modern look, sharpen up your sofa with a sharply tailored cover in plain white canvas. If you have an old leather chesterfield or an antique French daybed, its battered, worn look will only add to its charms, especially if you are going for a shabby-chic theme.

If you have retro tastes, you could trawl through eBay or visit car-boot sales to track down interesting 1960s or 1970s designs, although this calls for a certain amount of self-confidence and restraint, as there's a fine line between cool kitsch and completely naff.

OPPOSITE A display of children's drawings, portraits and artwork by family and friends creates a homely corner in an industrial-like space. The black floating shelf has been mounted at the same low level as a pile of Turkish floor cushions and features a flip-down front, fastened with hidden catches, that conceals everyday paraphernalia and unsightly electrical sockets/power outlets.

THIS PAGE In this converted shop, wood and leather combine to create a space that feels surprisingly warm and cosy despite the vast expanses of wall and floor. The 1950s armchair was found in the street and the owners decided to leave it outdoors to distress it naturally. The carpet is made from leather strips and the lamp is by Marcel Wanders for Moooi.

However, there is now a plethora of twentieth-century antiques shops and websites run by style-conscious retrophiles, where each and every piece has been carefully chosen by someone who really understands the look. For a really luxurious effect, if you have the space, invest in two sofas and add a couple of deep, squashy armchairs. Don't be afraid to mix the ultra-modern with the antique – the contrast will only add to the eclecticism of the Easy Elegance look.

Storage is another primary concern. If your sanctuary is to feel calm and peaceful, adopt a zero-tolerance strategy towards clutter. While you'll want to display personal treasures, more mundane and everyday items need to be stowed away out of sight yet kept within easy reach. Chimneybreast alcoves are a boon, as they provide a perfect home for fitted shelves. Opt for chunky shelving or trawl salvage yards for glazed doors that you can use to make doors on a built-in cupboard/ closet that will look as if it has always been there. Paint your cupboard doors for a clean, understated look, or strip them back to reveal layers of paint for a touch of Faded Elegance.

Sleek, low-level, mid-century sideboards are the ideal place to store photographs, old letters, CDs, DVDs and vinyl records, and the perfect choice if you are opting for a modern or retro look. They also provide a handy surface for a decorative arrangement of special treasures. Old metal travelling trunks can be used to store magazines or books while doubling up as side tables in a rustic living room, while old medical trolleys on castors make surprisingly stylish and conveniently mobile television stands.

ABOVE Sleek tailoring and a 1960s sideboard team up to create a chic interior full of depth and atmosphere. Different textures and tones of black and brown add definition. A Moroccan cushion provides a subtle injection of decorative detail – an ethnic reference repeated in the carved stone hand on the sideboard. Pink peonies introduce a hint of femininity.

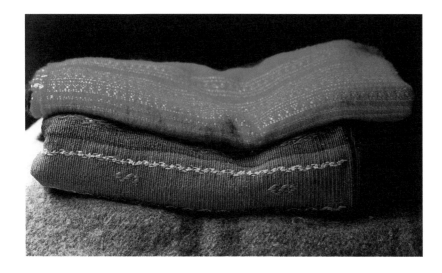

LEFT Mixing different styles and genres is a great way of creating a distinctive scheme. These ethnic fabrics clash in terms of colour, texture and pattern, yet the effect is unexpectedly pleasing, adding a truly individual statement to this room.

Sleek, low-level, mid-century sideboards are the ideal place to store photos, letters, CDs and vinyl records, and the perfect choice if you are going for a modern or retro look.

BELOW LEFT Luscious full-blown peonies casually arranged in a contemporary smoked-glass vase contrast beautifully with an antique stone carving.

BELOW RIGHT Matt and shiny surfaces work together to bring light and definition into this bold all-black scheme. Majestic violet delphiniums add some rich colour.

Lighting should be adaptable and practical, but with the huge variety of light fittings on offer it is also a great way of making a dramatic style statement. Chandeliers will add a glamorous note to any scheme. Good directional side lamps are a must for reading and casting ambient light at those times when overhead lighting feels too harsh.

The all-important finishing touches will allow your individuality to shine through. If you have many decorative items, group them together, leaving other areas of the room unadorned. This way the room won't feel too busy, and the display will have a stronger impact. For instance, a collection of antique plaster mouldings arranged on a mantelpiece in an otherwise spartan interior will create a focal point without overpowering the minimalist intent of the room, while a cluster of gilded mirrors hung together on one wall will make a bolder statement than if they were dotted about in a more traditional way.

BELOW LEFT AND RIGHT The simple decor provides a backdrop for an eclectic mix of furniture and accessories in this stylish living room. Modern, retro and ethnic pieces have been brought together to create a living space that's both fresh and lively.

OPPOSITE Warm neutral tones bring softness to a minimalist space and prevent it from feeling cold or austere. Floor-to-ceiling sliding glass doors flood the room with natural daylight that bounces off the polished-concrete floor. Retro leather sofas provide a comfortable place to rest and the mosaic-tile chimneybreast creates a textural focal point.

kitchens and dining rooms

THE KITCHEN IS USUALLY REGARDED AS THE HEART OF THE HOME, AND THE EASY ELEGANCE KITCHEN IS NO EXCEPTION.

Our increasingly busy lives mean that we make ever-greater demands on our kitchens. More often than not, kitchen and dining areas are now combined, as a lack of space and the trend towards a more relaxed style of entertaining have made the formal dining room almost obsolete. Bearing this in mind, think carefully about how you will use your kitchen. Obviously, the business of cooking and eating will take place there, but what about all the other activities, such as family gatherings, homework, filling in tax returns, dinner parties – even just relaxing?

One of the most important things to consider is storage. Insufficient cupboard space can detract from even the most elegant design, and in a kitchen, inevitably, there will be pots and pans, utensils, cutlery/flatware, china, glassware, appliances and foodstuffs to accommodate. But don't feel you have to rush to your nearest designer showroom and invest in a stereotypical built-in kitchen to house everything. Instead, think about the mood you want to evoke.

Do you yearn for a slick minimalist space where everything is concealed in sleek fitted cupboards with nothing left out on display, or would you feel more at home in the informal, cluttered atmosphere of a French country-style kitchen? If you are a serious cook, you may tend

LEFT Classic 1950s fibreglass dining chairs by Charles Eames work well with a chunky wooden table in this pared-down modern country home. Floor-to-ceiling sliding glass doors make the most of the view and blur the boundaries between the outdoors and inside.

OPPOSITE LEFT AND RIGHT Pistachio, lemon and baby-pink laminate doors create a harlequin effect in the kitchen of a renovated 1970s bungalow. Retro, industrial and country references combine to make a playful interior that's fresh and modern. The wooden work surfaces echo the ceiling beams, while aluminium pendant lights lend a utilitarian look.

towards the industrial feel of a professionally equipped kitchen, or perhaps you sympathize with the puritanical design ethic of the Shakers.

Once you have decided on the aesthetics, you can tackle the practicalities. A freestanding, deconstructed look will promote a relaxed atmosphere that's perfectly suited to the Easy Elegance ethos. Welsh dressers/hutches, butcher's blocks, former factory work benches or even an old chest of drawers refurbished with a marble top for kitchen use would all make suitable units and worksurfaces while contrasting stylishly with essential appliances such as refrigerators and cookers. If the notion of an unfitted kitchen appeals to you, be aware that freestanding cupboards tend to take up more

space and often don't hold quite as much as conventional units. One solution to storage in a freestanding kitchen is to devote one wall to a bank of floor-to-ceiling cupboards. Sleek flush doors with concealed catches create a streamlined look that's perfect for a modern space or to counterbalance the relaxed feel of the rest of the room, but if you want to add individuality to a slick, high-tech interior, look out for antique doors or shutters in a salvage yard or architectural antiques shop.

Most people's ideal would be to commission a tailormade kitchen to suit their own personal needs and space, but not everyone has that luxury. However, off-the-shelf units can be transformed with a little effort and imagination.

THIS PAGE AND OPPOSITE
Professional, stainless-steel catering
units make a sharp contrast with bare
brick walls in this farmhouse kitchen.
An old butcher's block is used as a
central island-cum-breakfast bar, and
a traditional range oven is set into
the chimneybreast.

ABOVE LEFT A set of Chippendale chairs take on a more casual feel when placed around a huge circular table in this rustic family dining room.

ABOVE RIGHT A mismatched collection of antique china, much of it in jewelled tones, stands out strongly against the drab-coloured paintwork of this vintage dresser/hutch.

Mass-produced frames can be customized by commissioning a carpenter to make doors to your own design or, simpler still, by hanging café-style curtains instead. Many people 'inherit' a kitchen that they can't afford to replace, or that's too good to rip out but is not to their taste. In this situation, give the room a makeover by adding glazed doors to wall cabinets so you can showcase china and glassware for a relaxed feel. Or hang open shelves and fit new worksurfaces to change the feel of the room.

Worksurfaces must be practical and hardwearing, but they also offer an opportunity to play around with the style elements of the space. There are no rules to say that you have to stick to one material throughout. Be bold, and combine wood with steel to add warmth to a hard-edged modern design; team marble and slate to add a touch of the French café look to a farmhouse-style kitchen; or couple Formica with enamel to break up the monotonous texture of laminate. Concrete is fun because it allows you to cast tops and units in one piece to create a smooth, tactile adobe-like finish that's reminiscent of a Provençal gîte or Santa Fe homestead.

Kitchen islands can be a real boon. Not only does an island provide additional storage and worksurfaces, but it also doubles as a

THIS PAGE In this elegant
kitchen, heritage paint colours,
enamelled terracotta Moroccan
wall tiles and a white range oven
all combine to create a look that
is surprisingly contemporary.
Faux-bamboo chairs introduce
a hint of faded grandeur, while
the Shaker-inspired cabinets
add utilitarian chic.

OPPOSITE Marble worktops, subway tiles and tongue-and-groove walls give this country kitchen a retro feel. ABOVE LEFT A double butler's sink is combined with sleek modern taps.

ABOVE RIGHT Glass storage jars hold colourful cake decorations. BELOW A mint-green retro-style fridge adds a splash of colour to a predominantly white kitchen.

breakfast bar or a place for guests to gather over a pre-dinner drink while you get on with the cooking. Match the island to the rest of your units or convert something unexpected like a science-lab workbench salvaged from an old school or a zinc-topped potting table to add a quirky touch. If space is an issue, opt for an island on wheels that can moved around the kitchen as needed.

Butler's sinks are timeless. Their chunky proportions and practical size gives them an enduring appeal. Old ones in good condition are fairly easy to come by, but new ones are virtually indistinguishable from the original models and kitchen companies are producing a host of modern versions that are well worth inspecting. If you are going for a traditional-style kitchen, then

OPPOSITE This simple kitchen design takes inspiration from different styles to create an eclectic look with earthy warmth. Subtle colours and the natural textures of wood, wicker, slate and plaster are offset by a high-tech stainless-steel cooker, while the antique Indian pillar adds an exotic twist. The chunky wooden shelves have been stained black to tie in with the slate floor and worktops.

RIGHT A huge stainless-steel range dominates this contemporary, Mediterranean-style kitchen. Open shelves and rustic wooden doors break up the long run of units, while limestone surfaces keep the scheme light and airy. The large kitchen island has been fitted with a dark wood top, adding another yet another dimension that keeps the overall look relaxed and informal.

BELOW These floating wooden shelves are laden with vintage china, earthenware and a number of quirky found objects, all in soft shades of white and cream.

old taps/faucets salvaged from hospitals or schools look great, but don't be fooled into thinking that they will be any cheaper than their modern cousins. Unless you want your new maple worktops ruined by leaks, you must get old taps/faucets fully reconditioned, which can end up costing the same as new state-of-the-art designer styles.

This also goes for appliances. Old 1950s fridges and cookers may look great, but they are not energy-efficient and can even be unsafe. Instead, look at the huge choice of modern retro-inspired models or, better still, opt for the hard-working appeal of professional catering equipment. These items will last a lifetime, cheerfully enduring just about anything a

LEFT A delicate bowl contrasts with the peeling paintwork of a wooden table.
BELOW AND OPPOSITE Decorative antiques sit side by side with retro pieces and industrial relics in this funky and eclectic dining area.

domestic situation can throw at them, and their no-nonsense utilitarian good looks will work well with all interior styles.

Unless you favour an ultra-minimalist look, you will want to display some of your favourite kitchen items. Plate racks or shelves are the ideal place for showing off decorative platters or bowls while a peg rail makes the perfect home for mugs. Don't forget that ordinary everyday china and utensils can also make pleasing arrangements. Vintage pots and pans hung on butcher's hooks from a metal rack suspended from the ceiling will add a rustic note, while stacks of plain white plates, bowls and pressed-glass tumblers look great when grouped together en masse. On the walls, display old wooden utensils or metal jelly-moulds in box frames, or group together five or six antique ceramic colanders hung on nails for a quirky effect.

Traditional dining rooms are rare these days, but efforts should be made to create a specific eating area, so that a casual midweek supper with friends can be treated with the ceremony that we tend to bestow only on celebratory meals. This doesn't need to involve starched napkins and silverware, but the aim should be to have a welcoming, comfortable zone that's suited to our modern way of living while still encompassing some of the pleasant formalities of old.

If you have a small kitchen, you coul dconsider knocking through a wall to the next room in order to create a dual-purpose space where cooking, eating and socializing become a shared experience. Few hosts want to feel as if they're shut away in the kitchen while their guests are having fun in the other room. And when it comes to choosing a table, go for the biggest model that fits comfortably. Don't be tempted to squeeze it into a corner in order to increase the sense of space. Instead, give your kitchen table pride of place and it will become the absolute centre of family life.

A plain refectory table is always a surefire success. Its generous dimensions make a bold statement, while its simple, clean lines and honest craftsmanship make it something of a style chameleon. A simple table can be dressed up with Gustavian cabriole-legged chairs for a feminine effect; team it with curvaceous Eames' dining chairs for a sensual yet modern look; choose curvy wrought-iron garden chairs for a whimsical country feel, or opt for long benches for chic, monastic simplicity.

Finally, for a retro theme, think about a sleek oval Ercol piece or a sculptural white Saarinen Tulip table. You can avoid any style typecasting by adding a surprising twist in the shape of weathered-oak blocks used as chunky stools, or perhaps a set of brushed-aluminium or Emeco 1006 Navy chairs, dating from the Second World War.

OPPOSITE AND ABOVE The occupants of this semi-industrial, open-plan living area have divided the space into distinct but freeflowing zones. A black-painted brick wall anchors the cooking and eating areas, while a stud wall, used to divide the kitchen and hallway, has had a slice taken out of it so that the two areas remain interconnected. A cowhide rug softens the concrete floors, and a long run of built-in cupboards has been customized with salvaged antique doors.

bedrooms

THE BEDROOM IS MORE THAN JUST A PLACE TO SLEEP – IT PROVIDES A REFUGE FROM THE BUSY, OFTEN CHAOTIC, WORLD OUTSIDE.

Because it's the most private room in the house, the bedroom is also the most personal, revealing much about the dreams and desires of its occupants. If you see the bedroom as your sanctuary, you can afford to be self-indulgent when it comes to the decoration.

Start planning your bedroom by considering the mood you would like to evoke in the room. Would you feel more relaxed in a stripped-back, minimalist space, or do you prefer a cosier feel, surrounded by the comforting clutter of personal treasures? What makes you feel calm and relaxed? Once you have made these important preliminary decisions, the rest will follow smoothly.

Traditionally, the bedroom has always been associated with soft, muted colours: chalky pastels, creamy whites and calm neutrals. These understated shades induce tranquillity, but calming tones such as charcoal, deep plum or olive green also create a soothing and soporific mood. Have fun introducing a splash of colour. An antique lace curtain, dyed slate grey, will add a sharper edge. Combine it with a bedhead upholstered in anthracite-coloured velvet and a few splashes of vivid fuchsia-pink in the form of cushions, as well as, for example, a treasured pair of emerald satin high-heels left out on display, and you have all the makings of a luxurious modern boudoir.

ABOVE Upholstered beds exude luxury and grandeur. This antique French example has been given an informal feel with a fresh pink and white spotted fabric.
OPPOSITE ABOVE LEFT Colourful costume jewellery is stored on a row of hooks.

OPPOSITE ABOVE RIGHT A pile of old books acts as a bedside table.
OPPOSITE BELOW RIGHT The owners of this room inherited the charming wallpaper when they bought the house.
OPPPOSITE BELOW LEFT A collection of perfume bottles adorn a metal table.

OPPOSITE An original 1960s evening gown makes a decorative display, while a white-painted bamboo table adds a simple, rustic note that tones down the opulence of this rather grand bedroom.

RIGHT AND FAR RIGHT The white-painted floorboards keep this modern-day boudoir from seeming too glitzy. The empty fireplace proves an unexpectedly convenient place to store a collection of pretty jewel-hued shoes.

Whatever style you have decided on – oriental boudoir, boutique-hotel chic, French country or a simple colonial style – the bed is the most important piece in the room.

If you revel in an invigorating environment, use a springlike palette of pretty pinks and leafy greens. Used sparingly in an all-white room with limewashed floorboards, these vibrant, dynamic shades offer the perfect backdrop for a fresh country-style bedroom.

Whatever style you have decided on, whether it be oriental boudoir, boutique-hotel chic, French country or a simple colonial style, the bed is without doubt the most important piece in the room. Choose your mattress with care, spending as much as your budget will allow. The bed frame or headboard, on the other hand, provides an opportunity to be more playful and indulgent. A four-poster will impart instant romance, whether

it be a Victorian wrought-iron bedstead or a sleek tubular-steel design – drape it in gauzy voile or an old linen sheet, or leave it bare to keep the look clean and unfussy.

For a touch of opulent frivolity, French eighteenth-century-style beds, either new or old, are perfect. Most of them have carved wood, caned or upholstered headboards and footboards that fit well with both a modern or traditional scheme. For something less elaborate, try hanging a fabric panel – a sari or a Moroccan wedding blanket would be ideal – or placing an old screen behind a divan bed for a simple but effective alternative. For an luxurious boutique-hotel feel, choose a tailored, padded headboard

LEFT Choosing a modern style in the bedroom doesn't mean you have to forfeit comfort and homeliness. This smart bedroom in a minimalist bungalow near the sea feels anything but cold and clinical.

OPPOSITE Khaki, plum, charcoal and sapphire make a striking colour scheme in a factory conversion. The bold jewel-like tones combine with the traditional elements of this inviting room to create a look that's modern and quirky.

covered in a sensual fabric such as washed linen, suede or velvet; tall proportions and button detailing will ensure that the finished product looks chic and up-to-date.

You will need somewhere to place your bedtime essentials: a book, glass of water and a reading lamp. Don't feel you have to match your bedside table to your bed. Instead, contrast old with new, futuristic with romantic, or industrial

with homely to keep the effect fresh and interesting. In an overtly feminine retreat, for instance, take the edge off potentially twee florals with a shot of the unexpected – a clear acrylic trolley or an injection-moulded plastic storage unit like Joe Colombo's Boby Trolley or Anna Castelli Ferrieri's Componibili stacking system will add just the right dose of modernism. Conversely, a scroll-legged, decorative gilt bedside

OPPOSITE AND BELOW LEFT Injections of
surprise are key to the Easy Elegance
look. This country bedroom benefits from
the introduction of a large-scale wallpaper
that rids the room of excessive prettiness.

BELOW RIGHT This curvy, rococo-style
bedhead and the elegant lamp lend an air
of sophistication to another beamed
bedroom in a country farmhouse.

table will prevent a minimalist or contemporary
bedroom from appearing clinical. Old metal café
tables, discarded wooden stools or abandoned
food trolleys all make innovative and quirky
bedside tables.

For a streamlined look with a nod to retro
styling, commission a carpenter to create a long,
low bedhead from laminated ply (there's an
amazing array of colours available), incorporating
integral shelves at the side to act as bedside
tables. Or create a bedside table with a touch of
1930s glamour by cladding the sides and top of a
plywood cube in bevelled mirrors, cut to size.

Storage, of course, is essential. Although
primarily for sleeping in, the bedroom also has to
house all your clothes, shoes, jewellery and bags,
and a tidy, clutter-free environment is far more
conducive to restful repose. Those with the
luxury of a spare room might consider
converting it into a dressing room lined with
hanging rails/rods, shelves and glass-fronted
drawers, but the majority of us have to conjure
up adequate space in our sleeping area. Antique
wardrobes/armoires create a stunning focal
point, but if you want your bed to take centre
stage, then a good solution is to create a faux
wall with hidden doors – panelling or tongue
and groove will help with the disguise – to
conceal a built-in storage system.

Favourite items can be left out on display, with
pretty hooks used to showcase floaty dresses or
sparkly necklaces. Don't dismiss the beauty of

everyday clothing either. You could hammer flat-headed nails into a wall in a grid formation, and hang a different-coloured linen shirt on each one to create a living wall sculpture that will change from day to day, depending on what you are wearing. Alternatively, create a wall of cubbyholes reminiscent of a school locker room, where jeans, T-shirts and cashmere jumpers can be neatly stacked. Paint the inside of each cubbyhole in a different shade to add interest.

Lighting is an important element in the bedroom. Downlighters tend to shine into your eyes when you are lying in bed, so opt for a central pendant or wall lights, making sure you fit a dimmer switch that allows you to adjust brightness levels to suit the mood. Crystal chandeliers and wall sconces create a soft, romantic feel, whether yours is a modern or traditional-style room. Antique examples have a vintage charm all of their own, but there are also numerous good-quality reproduction fittings to choose from. A bedside light is a must and, if you read in bed, a good adjustable task lamp, such as a classic anglepoise or a sleek halogen design, will prove invaluable.

Other bedroom essentials include a side chair, chaise longue or small sofa for lounging on or to act as an impromptu clothes horse, and a full-length mirror. Prop a huge gilded mirror against the wall for a grand statement or invest in a freestanding Edwardian-style cheval glass.

Window treatments should always reflect the character of the room. Rustic, cottage-style schemes, for example, look best with lightweight linens, simple cottons and diaphanous voiles hanging at the windows, while sensual boudoirs and grown-up, tailored rooms will benefit from

ABOVE A diaphanous 1930s tea dress hanging on an antique stripped-pine wardrobe may seem a homage to the country look, but the bamboo ladder and baskets give it a modern ethnic edge.
OPPOSITE Light and space are the true heroes in this Zen-like bedroom. A low bed makes the most of the bare plaster walls, while linen curtains diffuse the light for a soft, ethereal feel. An antique linen sheet acts as a bedspread, while velvet cushions and jewellery in a wooden bowl join forces to create a tactile and sensual oasis.

THIS PAGE AND OPPOSITE

A simple, pared-down space can be more conducive to sleep than an elaborately furnished room, as this plain, almost monastic bedroom, filled with only the bare essentials, clearly demonstrates. Two small and mismatched bedside tables – one a metal stool from an old factory and the other made from oddments of reclaimed wood – add texture to the room, while the specially forged bookshelf is the perfect place to stow current reading matter A metal Moroccan lantern has been suspended over one side of the bed to allow for late-night reading, and a vintage Canadian horse-blanket introduces an extra layer of warmth for the winter months. Careful accents of black add definition to the subtle colour scheme, while a small posy of flowers injects a vibrant shot of bright candy pink. The finished room possesses a considered austerity that feels calm and restful.

some theatrical drama in the shape of luxurious floor-to-ceiling curtains in heavy silk, velvet or linen.

When it comes to bedlinen, natural fabrics feel nicer against the skin and crisp white cotton and crumpled linen have a luxurious quality that can't be beaten. Romantic havens or rustic settings call for delicate threadwork pillowcases, embroidered duvet covers and checked blankets. For a contemporary feel, team chunky knits, satin throws and velvet cushions. An antique linen sheet dyed a colour that complements your scheme makes an ideal casual bedspread no matter what the style of your bedroom, while vintage eiderdowns will add a touch of retro homeliness.

bathrooms

INDULGE YOUR DECORATING FANTASIES AND CREATE A BATHROOM
THAT'S A HAVEN OF RELAXATION, BOTH PRACTICAL AND LUXURIOUS.

Throughout civilization, bathing has played a significant role in human lives, both physically and spiritually. Over the centuries, the rituals of washing and cleansing and the life-giving properties of water have been intrinsic parts of many different cultures and religions.

The first personal bathtub is thought to have been constructed around 1500 BC at the Palace of Knossos in Crete, but modern bathrooms owe more to the sanitary developments of the Victorian era – where daily ablutions were part of a dutiful routine rather than a therapeutic ritual – than to ancient times.

The Easy Elegance bathroom should be something of a sanctuary, where physical rejuvenation and sensory pleasure are every bit as important as clinical efficiency. When it comes to decorating, look past the obvious – tiled walls and matching bathroom suites – and consider a space that's more relaxed, a room that's comforting as well as functional. This can be achieved by introducing elements that are more usually found in other areas of the home. If space allows, a small daybed for lounging or an antique French wardrobe/armoire for storing towels and toiletries will add a touch of luxury. If your bathroom is on the small side, be creative. Chests of drawers can be cleverly adapted into a vanity unit without taking up any more room than a conventional example, while a small decorative

ABOVE AND OPPOSITE
The subued colours of this simple bathroom ensure a tranquil mood. Chalky walls, flaking paintwork and handmade tiles provide lots of tactile surfaces that make this space a sensual haven. The antique rolltop tub takes centre stage, giving a sense of luxury, while

diaphanous linen curtains gently filter the light. Untreated floorboards are a practical solution underfoot, and reclaimed doors have been turned into a built-in cupboard to conceal the boiler and to store towels. An old ladder has a new life as a towel rail, and a shell makes a pretty soap dish.

Deca

OPPOSITE A bold use of black gives this stylish bathroom a theatrical feel. A 1930s mirrored side table adds glamour and sparkle while serving as the perfect place for toiletries and other essentials. An antique linen tablecloth, dyed charcoal grey, hangs at the window, held back with a plump jute tassel. THIS PAGE Decorative details bring personality and interest to a bathroom scheme and can help to reinforce the overall atmosphere. Bowls of assorted shells and pieces of coral, pretty scented soaps, a simple vase of flowers or rows of old glass apothecary jars are ideal for adding those all-important finishing touches.

If you are lucky enough to have a bathroom of generous proportions, a freestanding tub has a regal quality that will make bathtime feel both luxurious and ceremonial.

side table could be squeezed in alongside the bathtub to hold soaps, books and lotions and potions. If the idea of blurring the boundaries in this way appeals to you, you could also consider incorporating a freestanding bathtub into your bedroom for a self-indulgent bathing experience. The idea is to create your own individual spa, somewhere you can enjoy a brief period of solitude.

Choosing the colour scheme is a good place to start, as it will set the tone for the room's mood and feel. White is an obvious choice if you like a light, fresh environment, but it can feel cold and clinical. Temper it with pale, washed-out

ABOVE A pair of basins has been set into a floating shelf complete with a slot from which to hang a hand towel. BELOW A worn wooden block and tiny round tiles lend softness to an all-white bathroom.

blues and greys for a cool beachy look, soft neutrals for a more sophisticated note, or chalky pastels for a subtle touch of femininity. Gauzy sheers or frosted glass at the windows will make the most of the available natural daylight. However, you may prefer a more muted atmosphere – think of a Turkish bath or Moroccan hammam – in which case, choose from a colour palette based on earthy browns and burnished metallics. Indian fretwork shutters or Venetian blinds/shades can control the daylight, allowing it through in dramatic shafts to enhance the mood.

The walls should reflect the overall style of the room. Brick-shaped glazed subway tiles in pastel shades of palest aqua or primrose yellow are ideal if you are opting for a slightly retro-style scheme, while handmade terracotta tiles have an attractively uneven tone and surface that is perfect if you want to add texture to your interior. Don't be afraid to experiment with different wall coverings. Flamboyant wallpaper (make sure it is suitable for bathroom use) can create a sexy boudoir effect, or you could strip the walls to reveal flaked paint or crumbling plaster for a Faded Elegance look. Georgian-style panelling will suggest a gentleman's club ambience and makes a striking contrast to sleek modern fittings.

In a bathroom, the inevitable water spillages and damp conditions means that floor coverings must be practical. Wooden floorboards are inexpensive, warm underfoot and non-slip, but if you

THIS PAGE A huge modern shower rose promises a luxurious drenching in this sleek, walk-in shower tiled with chic, elongated black ceramic tiles. Frosted-glass doors offer privacy without blocking out the natural daylight.

OPPOSITE AND BELOW LEFT This elegant bathroom demonstrates an ingenious use of space. A half-frosted glass wall divides the shower and bath, creating two rooms in one. A plastic trolley offers extra storage.

BELOW RIGHT Pale green mosaic tiles give this wet room a slightly municipal retro appeal, while the limestone shower tray and coordinating basin bring a contemporary aspect to the room.

want a more polished, sleek look, then opt for stone or slate tiles (you may need underfloor heating in colder climates), which will give you the glossy effect you seek.

The most important piece in the bathroom is the bathtub. If you are lucky enough to have a bathroom of generous proportions, a freestanding bathtub has a regal quality that will make bathtime feel both luxurious and ceremonial. Rolltop tubs, with their sensuous curves, make a stunning statement in any scheme. Hunt out old claw-footed versions in salvage yards or antique bathroom specialists, or choose

a reproduction model. Alternatively you may prefer to try to recreate the simplistic purity of a Japanese sento with a cedarwood soaking tub, which releases its aromatic scent while you wallow in the water, or the monastic minimalism favoured by designers such as Philippe Starck, whose renowned Starck 1 bathroom collection was inspired by the shape of the humble water pail. However, in a small bathroom, a space-saving built-in bathtub is the best solution. House it behind a panel of reclaimed floorboards for a contemporary country look, or cover the panel with tiny mosaic tiles for a modern hammam feel.

ABOVE LEFT A sense of space and vast expanses of white save this candyfloss-pink bath and polka-dot wallpaper from looking too sugary. An oriental lantern introduces a splash of bold colour and a geisha twist to the scheme.

TOP RIGHT A vintage Lloyd Loom chair offers a comfortable spot to sit while waiting for the bath to fill.
ABOVE RIGHT A rose-tinted vintage glass dish is used as a soap dish.
OPPOSITE For most of us, rolltop tubs are the height of bathing

luxury, and this extra-deep, double-ended example offers just that. White floorboards, tongue-and-groove walls and a vintage metal café table are practical additions that contribute to the room's pretty country feel.

ABOVE AND ABOVE RIGHT A simple bentwood stool strikes a contemporary note in this pared-down bathroom. Brick-shaped subway tiles provide old-fashioned charm and a gauzy blind controls the light. An old wooden bath-rack is a practical solution in the absence of a side ledge or bath surround.

Alternatively, you could opt for ever-useful and practical tongue-and-groove panelling, which is versatile enough to fit in with almost any style you are aiming for.

When it comes to the sink, don't feel you must match it to the bathtub – a juxtaposition of different styles is at the heart of Easy Elegance. Combine a cast-iron or copper Napoleonic-style slipper bath with the clean lines of a contemporary sink; create a focal point in an understated modern bathroom by introducing an Edwardian marble vanity unit; or add a dash of Hollywood glamour to a shabby-chic washroom in the shape of a majestic Art Deco powder-blue pedestal sink. Bathroom sinks also offer a great opportunity to make a style statement. Showcase the clean edges of a limestone basin by placing it on an ornate, marble-topped gilt console table for a truly one-off addition to a scheme. Or, for a recycled effect, construct a homespun console-style washstand using reclaimed scaffolding poles and weathered planks.

ABOVE AND ABOVE LEFT This unusual bathroom is a successful mixture of rustic, modern and antique ingredients that come together to create a look full of charm and character. Rough-hewn logs make a window ledge, while the contemporary basin contrasts with the claw-footed iron tub.

There is nothing like being drenched in a good hot shower. If you can find the space for a wet room, so much the better. Tile it in tiny mosaic squares in watery shades of turquoise and palest green to conjure up memories of old-fashioned public swimming baths, or go for a modern-day Turkish-bath feel, using deeper shades like indigo, bronze or even black.

To help maintain a feeling of calm and serenity, good storage is a must. Built-in cabinets, old linen presses or even a 1960s sideboard will all provide space for bath linen and toiletries, but if space is at a premium, be inventive. Luggage rails, salvaged from decommissioned trains, are perfect for holding towels. Traditional apple racks can hold copious amounts of make-up and lotions while taking up the minimum amount of floor-space, and an old kitchen corner cupboard could find a new lease of life in the bathroom. Glass jars make ideal containers for soaps and cotton wool, while French shopping baskets, hung from rows of decorative hooks, can help accommodate the overflow.

workrooms

MAKE WORK MORE OF A PLEASURE BY CREATING A DEDICATED SPACE THAT IS AN ELEGANT AND EFFICIENT WORKING ENVIRONMENT.

Working from home, ploughing through household paperwork or merely enjoying a favourite hobby – these activities all demand a quiet corner where we can devote ourselves to our endeavours. Any job is more pleasant if it takes place in a calm and ordered space that is well suited to its purpose. The Easy Elegance workroom is a relaxed, personal space, both inspiring and organized, where you can get to grips with your day-to-day tasks, be they writing letters or keeping up with studying, arranging flowers, doing the ironing, or even closing multi-million dollar deals.

With technology and communications improving all the time, working from home is becoming increasingly popular and increasingly common, as people attempt to escape impersonal office environments and the grind of commuting. A wireless laptop computer is a great space-saving investment as it is small and compact and completely mobile, meaning you can set up camp on the sofa or any available tabletop. However, the ideal situation is to convert a whole room into a permanent office space, because this allows you to work free from distraction, to spread out and not to have to

THIS PAGE Books line the walls on floor-to-ceiling shelves made from old railway sleepers/railroad ties in this cosy study. An antique garden chair is paired with a faded country table, and an old fruit crate underneath is used to store paper. The only concession to modernity is the slick task lamp on the table.

OPPOSITE LEFT AND RIGHT A wide curved shelf acts as a desk on the landing of the top floor in a family townhouse. Vintage haberdashery boxes sit beside files housing paperwork, ribbons and other essentials needed by its creative occupant. Postcards and photos are casually pinned to the wall, and a red chair adds a dash of colour.

OPPOSITE BELOW RIGHT A montage of photos, drawings and souvenirs offers inspiration in this designer's work space.

clear everything away at the end the day. If devoting an entire room to a workroom is not a possibility, you may be able to squeeze a tiny office under the stairs or on a landing. Alternatively, you could commission a modern secretaire for a corner of your living room, or source an antique one.

The style and decoration of a workroom is hugely important. A beautiful, cohesive scheme will have a calming effect that promotes efficiency, productivity and, of course, creativity. Pale neutral colours are generally accepted to be tranquil and unchallenging and thus to offer a suitable backdrop for work spaces. However, don't shy away from bolder colours if they inspire you. A sage-green office offers a serene yet stimulating backdrop, as long as it is

BELOW LEFT Pretty Victorian brackets and a cut-down scaffolding plank create an ingenious shelf. **BELOW CENTRE** Antique metal brackets can be used decoratively. **BELOW RIGHT** A stack of antique grain sacks waits to be converted into cushion covers.

OPPOSITE This rustic cabin is a creative retreat. A discarded metal factory workbench has found a new life as a desk, while the vintage machinist's chair has been covered in fresh floral cotton. A simple lace panel at the window softens the edges of this utilitarian space.

contrasted with lots of clean-lined, white-painted furniture, while deeper shades such as mink grey or French blue can create a womb-like space that is conducive to deep thought. If you like to amass postcards, magazine tear-sheets, newspaper clippings or snippets of fabric, a large noticeboard will be useful. Cover a large piece of fibreboard or cork in thick felt or linen to create a blank canvas for all your visual references, and you may just end up with an arrangement of images that's a work of art in itself.

When arranging a workroom or home office, consider how you like to work, and choose your desk accordingly. The general rule is the bigger,

the better. If you tend to think more clearly on your feet, look for a waist-high workbench. A stool or an old factory machinist's chair can provide a welcome place to perch upon when your legs get tired.

Wood is a warmer and more comfortable surface to work on than metal or glass, and can be adapted to suit many styles. An old carpenter's bench would be perfect for a workshop feel, while painted floorboards resting on a couple of trestles would fit into a contemporary country look, and a 1950s laminate-topped kitchen table hints at retro-style domestic bliss. If you are after a slick, high-tech

LEFT A metal hanging rail/rod runs the length of this simple utility room, providing plenty of space to hang the ironing. The wooden shelf displays pretty antique china, and an old-fashioned cane carpet-beater hangs on the back of the door.
OPPOSITE LEFT A large glass-fronted cupboard, housing empty jam jars and vases, dominates this utility room. A row of decorative hooks holds coats and hats, while a basket keeps shoes and boots tidily tucked away.
OPPOSITE RIGHT An old earthenware sink has been set on top of a stand made from chunky reclaimed wood in this old-fashioned scullery. Cleaning equipment, kitchen utensils and gardening tools are stored side by side, making this room a multi-purpose space.

workspace, there are plenty of excellent contemporary designs around. Better still, have a desk custom-made to your own requirements and paint it with high-gloss white for a coolly futuristic look, or go for something more natural like khaki or taupe for contemporary chic.

A good work chair must first and foremost be comfortable. If you spend all day, every day sitting at a desk, it is well worth investing in an ergonomic design that offers excellent lumbar support. If you have opted for a faded, distressed look or a simple country theme and are worried that a modern, high-tech piece of furniture will clash, remember that a bold contrast can keep your look lively and fresh.

However, forget the ubiquitous polypropylene chairs that are found in office-supply stores and instead opt for something that looks every bit as good as it feels. Design classics by icons such as Vico Magistretti and Charles Eames are still in

production, and originals can be picked up in auctions and from twentieth-century antique dealers, while modern designers such as Jasper Morrison and Ross Lovegrove are busy turning out functional, stylish and up-to-date office furniture that would work well in any interior.

In a workroom, good organization is a must. Tailor your storage to suit your needs. In a utility room, an old linen press would be the perfect place to stow stacks of bedding, while Shaker-style peg rails make ideal resting places for brooms, brushes and ladders. If this functional style is not to your taste, full-height cupboards covering a whole wall will provide a vast amount of storage and keep a room calm and entirely clutter-free. Touch catches and secret hinges will keep the look minimal. Alternatively, old school lockers, a set of antique spice drawers or even abandoned fruit crates can contain all manner of papers and other office paraphernalia.

outdoor spaces

DURING THE SUMMER MONTHS, TURN YOUR OUTSIDE SPACE INTO AN EXTENSION OF YOUR INTERIOR – RELAXED, INVITING AND PRACTICAL.

Think of your outdoor space as an extension of your interior. Whatever your little patch of the outside world consists of – rolling green acres, a postage-stamp-sized city garden, a tiny balcony or a rooftop terrace – you will need to apply the same principles and pay the same attention to its design and arrangement as you do to the interior of your home, furnishing it with tables, chairs, cushions, lighting and decorative accessories.

If you have a covered verandah or porch, make the most of the space and use it to create an outside living room, complete with wicker sofa, armchairs and side tables, where you can entertain during the warmer months. Hang pictures and mirrors on the walls and drape them with tiny twinkling fairy lights. A gazebo at the end of the garden can be decked out with a table, chairs, hanging candelabra, and even rush matting underfoot. Wicker armchairs with plump cushions are perfect for reading or snoozing in the sun. Aim to create a relaxed, comfortable space that feels like a real room where you can relax, eat, entertain friends or simply sit and read.

The architecture of your home and the type of outdoor space you have will influence the mood, style and decorative theme. A cottage calls for a rambling country garden filled with scented roses, sweet-pea wigwams and antique metal furniture, whereas a glass-fronted, modern bungalow will demand architectural plants and

ABOVE A covered verandah is the perfect place to create an outdoor dining room for the summer months. Here, an array of mismatched furniture has been unified with white paint, while blue-and-white-striped cushions soften the seats. Hanging lanterns are suspended from a pair of weather-worn antlers and cotton bunting gives a festive feel.

OPPOSITE A simple hammock is piled with vintage cushions and a cosy blanket to create a welcoming spot in the shade for a post-lunch nap. The addition of a metal candelabrum is a quirky decorative touch.

OPPOSITE An old outhouse has been transformed into a rustic garden room. Old wooden sieves adorn the planked walls and the buckets of loose country flowers keep the effect fresh and pretty. **RIGHT** A delicate wirework planter holds geraniums and hydrangeas in a flagstoned porch. **ABOVE RIGHT** Metal laundry tubs and galvanized metal buckets have been given a second life as plant pots in this cottage garden. **BELOW RIGHT** A wicker sofa dressed with floral and gingham cushions has been placed in a shady corner of the garden to offer a welcome retreat on a hot summer day.

A charming cottage naturally calls for a rambling country garden filled with old-fashioned scented roses, sweet-pea wigwams and antique metal garden furniture.

slick contemporary pieces. However, as always, contrast and surprise are key to Easy Elegance, so don't be afraid to mix and match different style elements, perhaps combining a contemporary metal table with rusting French café chairs, or placing a pair of slick modern sunloungers in front of an elegant Georgian townhouse, and thus keeping the outside of your home as fresh and lively as the inside.

One of the main components of a successful outside room is some sort of permanent structure within which to arrange your furnishings. Such a structure will help to delineate the space, while offering some protection from the forces of nature. An existing fence, wall or outbuilding will suffice, but you can also

ABOVE LEFT AND RIGHT Moroccan lanterns hang from the mature grape vine that shades this charming Parisian courtyard. A dainty wrought-iron table and chairs provide a place to enjoy an intimate meal on a summer's evening, while decorative pots filled with fragrant herbs line up along the wall.

improvise. Woven willow panels, available from garden centres, offer a quick, easy and relatively inexpensive way to put together an ad-hoc outdoor sitting area, or you could even think about investing in a former army mess tent or a canvas dining shelter with sides that roll down for an even more enclosed feel.

Eating al fresco is indisputably one of life's greatest pleasures. Those living in warmer climates will accept this as a natural part of their day-to-day life, but for those of us who reside in chillier regions, it's something to be looked forward to all winter – and that first dinner outside, on a balmy summer evening, is one of the highlights of the year.

However small your outside space, you must make room for a table and chairs, but at all costs avoid the cheap (and uncomfortable) moulded plastic furniture found in garden centres. If your budget is limited, scour junk shops for old

ABOVE LEFT AND RIGHT Original Antelope chairs by Ernest Race are teamed with a rusty antique folding metal table in this quaint glasshouse. Rows of seedlings on the window sill await repotting, while in the corner young cucumbers are growing in a disused galvanized-metal bathtub.

decorator's tables or fold-up metal ones, or you could even lay an old door across two trestles. Old-fashioned slatted wooden chairs that might have been seen in a 1920s cricket pavilion and decommissioned Parisian park benches look charming (add plenty of cushions for comfort) and are classic enough to work within any garden scheme, while chunky sawn logs are a brilliant outdoor accessory and can serve as impromptu stools, side tables or plant stands.

When it comes to accessories, decorate your outdoor dining area with hanging paper lanterns, cotton bunting and glass storm lanterns. A strategically hung mirror will introduce a dash of glamour while helping to create the illusion of more space in a small area.

Just as an interior feels naked without fresh flowers, no patio or terrace would be complete without some planted-up containers. If you are going for terracotta pots, invest in good-quality

frost-resistant ones. Tone down new terracotta by brushing on a thin layer of watered-down yogurt, which will soon encourage the growth of lichen, with its beautiful green tinge. Fill your pots with aromatic plants such as lavender, rosemary, jasmine and nicotiana, all of which will fill the evening air with seductive scent.

This is an area of the garden where you can really unleash your creativity and invent planters from all manner of different items. Old galvanized metal tubs and buckets can be filled with salad leaves (drill holes in the bottom for drainage before you fill them) and placed outside your back door as an attractive and convenient miniature herb or kitchen garden. Keep an eye open at salvage yards for old enamel pails, chipped ceramic butler's sinks, agricultural drinking troughs and laundry tubs, all of which make brilliant and unexpected planters. Or you could consider commissioning something to your own design. Old railway sleepers/railroad ties, corrugated-iron or zinc sheeting could all be adapted to create unique and stylish planters.

If you are fortunate enough to have the space, a small writer's retreat or artist's studio right at the bottom of the garden is a wonderful idea. A simple garden shed wired up for electricity is enough, but if you want to be really adventurous you could set up camp in an old shepherd's hut or gypsy caravan or, for some serious retro cool, invest in a sleek vintage American Airstream trailer or even an old VW Kombi van.

ABOVE Lush green foliage stands out against a black-painted fence on this urban roof terrace. A large weathered table sits in the centre surrounded by a set of utilitarian galvanized metal chairs. The pair of bamboo lanterns on the table wait to be lit as dusk falls.

OPPOSITE Floor-to-ceiling sliding glass doors give an uninterrupted view through this modernist bungalow to the woods beyond. They can be completely opened on hot days to make the connection between indoors and oudoors even stronger.

resources

UK RESOURCES

ANTIQUES

Cornucopia
12 Upper Tachbrook Street
London SW1 1SH
020 7828 5752
www.cornucopiaantiques-
collectables.co.uk
Vintage textiles.

The Dining Room Shop
62–64 White Hart Lane
London SW13 0PZ
020 8878 1020
www.thediningroomshop.co.uk
*China, glassware, cutlery and
furniture.*

Glass Etc.
18–22 Rope Walk
Rye
East Sussex TN31 7NA
01797 226600
www.decanterman.com
Antique glassware

Pimpernel & Partners
596 Kings Road
London SW6 2DX
020 7731 2448
www.pimpernelandpartners.co.uk
Antique furniture and mirrors.

Retro Sixty
10 Oakwood Drive
Bramley Green, Angmering
West Sussex BN16 4GB
(showroom by appointment
only)
07841 535864
www.retrosixty.co.uk
Twentieth-century furniture.

Josephine Ryan Antiques
17 Langton Street
London SW10 0JL
020 7352 5618
www.Josephineryanantiques.co.uk
*Chandeliers, antique mirrors,
furniture and accessories.*

Strand House
The Strand
Rye
East Sussex TN31 7DB
01797 224002
*Old leather armchairs, sofas,
chaises and antique mirrors.*

**Twentieth Century
Antiques**
Edinburgh
07715 120133
www.twentiethcenturyantiques.
co.uk
Twentieth-century modern design.

SALVAGE &
RECLAMATION

The House Hospital
14a Winders Road
London SW11 3HE
010 7223 3179
www.thehousehospital.com
*Architectural salvage, from baths
and basins to radiators and
fireplaces.*

Lassco
Brunswick House
30 Wandsworth Road
London SW8 2LG
020 7394 2100
www.lassco.co.uk
*Old doors, pillars, flooring and
household fixtures and fittings.*

Retrouvious
1016 Harrow Road
London NW10 5NS
020 8960 6060
www.retrouvious.com
Architectural salvage and design.

Walcot Reclamation
Tyning Road
Bathampton
Bath
Avon BA2 6TQ
01225 469557
www.walcot.com
*Reclaimed flooring, oak beams
and wooden panelling.*

HOMEWARE

Atelier Abigail Ahern
137 Upper Street
London N1 1Qp
020 7354 8181
www.abigailahern.com
A quirky mix of accessories.

**The Atlantic Blanket
Company**
0845 6585194
www.atlanticblankets.com
Gorgeous blankets and throws.

Baileys Home and Garden
Whitecross Farm
Bridstow
Herefordshire HR9 6JU
01989 561931
www.baileyshomeandgarden.
com
*Homeware and furniture
inspired by reclaimed objects.*

The Big Tomato Company
0208 968 1815
www.bigtomatocompany.com
*English creamware with attitude,
including designs by Atlanta
Bartlett.*

David Coote
01797 344077
www.davidcoote.co.uk
*Interiors and furniture made
using reclaimed materials.*

Emery et Cie
020 8969 0222
www.emeryetcie.com
Eclectic pieces for the home.

The French House
41–43 Parsons Green Lane
London SW6 4HH
020 7371 7573
www.thefrenchhouse.co.uk
*Fabulous stock of antiques and
20th-century furniture.*

Hotspot Blinds
01394 388573 (British agent)
www.nature-deco.de
or 0336093815 (Germany)
*Contemporary and classic blinds
for the modern home.*

I Gigi
31a & 37 Western Road
Hove
East Sussex BN3 1AF
01273 775257
www.igigigeneralstore.com
*Designer, traditional and global
items for the home and person.*

John Lewis
www.johnlewis.com
*The classic one-stop shop for
good-quality, well-designed
homeware.*

The Laundry
01594 841824
www.thelaundry.co.uk
*Beautiful 1930s- to 1950s-
inspired bed linen and
household textiles.*

Nicole Farhi Homeware
115 Fulham Road
London SW3 6RL
020 7838 0937
www.nicolefarhi.com
*Furniture and accessories for
the home.*

Ochre
020 7096 7372 (UK)
001 212 414 4332 (US)
www.ochre.net
*Contemporary yet timeless
furniture, lighting and
accessories.*

Pale & Interesting
01797 344077
www.paleandinteresting.com
*A capsule collection of furniture,
accessories and jewellery made
from vintage materials by
Atlanta Bartlett and David
Coote.*

**The Shop Next Door
at The George in Rye**
96 High Street
Rye
East Sussex, TN31 7JT
01797 228626
Decorative homewares.

Toast
0844 55785200
www.toast.co.uk
Beautiful items for the home.

The White Company
www.thewhitecompany.com
*Fine quality bed linen, towels
and home furnishings.*

LIGHTING
Artemide
106 Great Russell Street
London WC1B 3NB
www.artemide.com
Sleek modern lighting.

Hector Finch Lighting
90 Wandsworth Bridge Road
London SW6 2TF
020 7731 8886
www.hectorfinch.com
Antique and repro lighting.

London Lighting
135 Fulham Road
London SW3 6RT
020 7589 3612
www.londonlighting.co.uk
Designer lighting.

FURNITURE
Aria
Barnsbury Hall
Barnsbury Street
London N1 1PN
020 7704 6222
www.aria-shop.co.uk
Modern furniture emporium.

Bed Bazaar
The Old Station, Station Road
Framlingham
Suffolk IP13 9EE
01728 72756
www.bedbazaar.co.uk
Antique bedsteads.

The French Bed Company
01799 542358
www.thefrenchbedcompany.co.uk
Beds with a romantic feel.

George Smith Sofas
587–589 Kings Road
London SW6 2EH
020 7384 1004
www.georgesmith.co.uk
Traditional upholstered furniture.

Sasha Waddell Furniture
020 8979 9189
www.sashawaddell.co.uk
*Scandinavian-style painted
furniture.*

SCP
135–139 Curtain Road
London EC2A 3BX
020 7739 1869
www.scp.co.uk
Modern British furniture.

Skandium
86 Marylebone High Street
London W1U 4QS
020 7935 2077
www.skandium.com
*Contemporary Scandinavian
design.*

Vitsoe
72 Wigmore Street
London W1U 2SG
020 7935 4968
www.vitsoe.com
Modern shelving systems.

TEXTILES &
WALLPAPER
Cabbages and Roses
3 Langton Street
London SW10 0JL
020 7352 7333
www.cabbagesandroses.com
Faded florals by the metre.

Cole & Son
Lifford House
199 Eade Road
London N4 1DN
020 8442 8844
www.cole-and-son.com
Fine hand-printed wallpapers.

Colefax and Fowler
110 Fulham Road
London SW3 6HU
0207244 7427
www.colefax.com
*Traditional and contemporary
English fabrics and wallpapers.*

Neisha Crosland
8 Elystan Street
London SW3 3NS
020 7584 7988
www.neishacrosland.com
Contemporary prints.

MacCulloch & Wallis
25–26 Dering Street
London W1S 1AT
020 7629 0311
www.macculloch-wallis.co.uk
Fine fabrics and trimmings.

Ian Mankin
271–273 Wandsworth
   Bridge Road
London SW6 2TX
020 7722 0997
www.ianmankin.co.uk
Canvas, ticking, cotton and linen.

EW Moore & Son
39–43 Plashet Grove
London E6 1AD
020 8471 9392
www.ewmoore.com
*A selection of vintage
wallpapers.*

Rosie's Vintage Wallpaper
www.rosiesvintagewallpaper.com
*Vast collection of vintage
wallpapers.*

Johnny Tapete
0049 201 6124647
www.vintage-wallpaper.com
Supplier of vintage wallpaper.

Whaleys (Bradford) Ltd
01274 576718
www.whaleys-bradford.ltd.uk
*Cotton, linen, canvas, twill and
muslin.*

KITCHENS &
BATHROOMS
Alternative Plans
4 Hester Road
London SW11 4AN
0207228 6460
www.alternative-plans.co.uk
Contemporary designs.

Habitat
www.habitat.net
Freestanding kitchens.

Plain English
28 Blandford Street
London W1U 4BZ
020 7486 2674
www.plainenglishdesign.co.uk
Handcrafted bespoke kitchens.

The Water Monopoly
16–18 Lonsdale Road
London NW6 6RD
020 7624 2636
www.watermonopoly.com
Restored antique sanitaryware.

PAINT
Farrow and Ball
www.farrow-ball.com
Heritage paint colours.

The Paint Library
5 Elystan Street
London SW3 3NT
020 7823 7755
www.paintlibrary.co.uk
*Contemporary paints and
wallpapers.*

Papers and Paints
4 Palk Walk
London SW10 0AD
020 7352 8626
www.papers-paints.com
Custom-blended colours.

GARDENS & FLOWERS
John Austin Roses
Bowling Green Lane
Albrighton
Wolverhampton WV7 3HB
01902 376300
www.davidaustinroses.co.uk
English garden roses.

Europlus Adventure
Supplies
Haynes West End
Bedford MK45 3QU
01234 740327
www.canvastentshop.co.uk
*Army-style tents and utility
camping equipment.*

The Indian Garden
Company
01491 628584
www.indiangardencompany.
co.uk
*Exotic textiles, umbrellas and
hand-crafted accessories for the
garden.*

The Real Flower
Company
01730 818300
www.realflowers.co.uk
Garden roses by post.

Petersham Nurseries
Off Petersham Road
Richmond
Surrey TW10 7AG
*Stylish nursery with highly
acclaimed restaurant attached.*

US RESOURCES

ANTIQUES & VINTAGE
ABC Carpet & Home
888 Broadway
New York, NY 10003
(212) 473-3000
www.abchome.com
*Antique and contemporary
furnishings, linens, rugs, and
other accessories.*

English Country Antiques
Snake Hollow Road
Bridgehampton, NY 11932
(516) 537-0606
www.ecantiques.com
*Period country furniture and
decorative accessories.*

Herman Miller Inc.
(616) 654 3860
www.hermanmiller.com
Fine twentieth-century furniture.

Howard Kaplan Antiques
827 Broadway
New York, NY 10003
(212) 674-1000
www.howardkaplanantiques.
com
*French antiques and
reproductions.*

Moss
146 Greene Street
New York, NY 10012
(212) 226 2190
*Original and reproduction
pieces.*

Sage Street Antiques
Sage Street (off Route 114)
Sag Harbor, NY
(631) 725-4036
Period furniture and accessories.

Therien and Company
716 North La Cienega
Boulevard
Los Angeles, CA 90069
(310) 657-4615
www.therien.com
Period antique furniture.

20CDesign.com
1430 N Riverfront Blvd.
Dallas, TX 75207
(214) 939-1430
www.20Cdesign.com
Classic modern furniture.

Unica Home
3901 West Russell Road
Las Vegas, NV 89118
(888) 89-UNICA
www.unicahome.com
*Modern furniture and
accessories, both vintage and
reproductions.*

FURNITURE
Conran Shop
415 East 59th Street
New York, NY 10022
(212) 755 7249
www.conran.com
*Arne Jacobsen and Verner
Panton furniture and Le Klint
lamps.*

Crate & Barrel
(800) 996-9960
www.crateandbarrel.com
*Clean, contemporary furniture
and accessories.*

Design Within Reach
(800) 944-2233
www@dwr.com
*Authentic 20th-century design
classics sold online and from
studios across the country.*

IKEA
(800) 434-4532
www.ikea.com
*Simple but well-designed
furniture plus inexpensive
storage and kitchenware
solutions.*

Jennifer Convertibles
www.jenniferfurniture.com
Sleeper sofas and armchairs.

Pier One Imports
(212) 206-1911
www.pier1.com
*Home accessories and furniture
from all over the world.*

Pottery Barn
(800) 922-5507
www.potterybarn.com
*Elegant furniture and
accessories.*

West Elm
www.westelm.com
*Contemporary furniture and
accessories.*

SALVAGE &
RECLAMATION
Caravati's Inc.
104 East Second Street
Richmond, VA 23224
(804) 232-4175
Restoration materials.

Cleveland Wrecking
3170 East Washington
Boulevard
Los Angeles, CA 90023
(213) 269-0633
General salvage.

Florida Victorian
Architectural Antiques
112 West Georgia Avenue
Deland, FL 32724
(904) 734-9300
www.floridavictorian.comß
*Nineteenth- and early
twentieth-century architectural
elements.*

Salvage One
1524 South Sangamon Street
Chicago, IL 60608
(312) 733-0098
General salvage.

United House
Wrecking, Inc.
535 Hope Street
Stamford, CT 06906
(203) 348-5371
General salvage.

KITCHENS & BATHROOMS

The Antique Hardware Store
19 Buckingham Plantation Drive
Bluffon, SC 29910
(800) 422-9982
Unusual and antique hardware.

P. E. Guerin, Inc.
21–23 Jane Street
New York, NY 10014
(212) 243-5270
www.peguerin.com
Decorative hardware.

Quintessentials
532 Amsterdam Avenue
New York, NY 10024
(212) 877-1919 or
(888) 676-BATH
www.qkb.com
Quality hardware.

Restoration Hardware
(800) 910-9836
www.restorationhardware.com
Hardware, home furnishings, lighting, and accessories for the home.

Vintage Plumbing
9645 Sylvia Avenue
Northridge, CA 91324
(818) 772-1721
www.vintageplumbing.com
Original and restored bathroom antiques, including clawfoot tubs.

Waterworks
(800) 998-BATH
www.waterworks.com
Bathroom and kitchen fixtures.

LIGHTING

Ann Morris Antiques
239 East Sixtieth Street
New York, NY 10022
(212) 755-3308
Fine reproduction lamps and shades.

Boyd Lighting
Brass Light Gallery
131 South First Street
Milwaukee, WI 53204
(800) 243-9595
Traditional and contemporary fixtures.

Eron Johnson Antiques, Ltd.
451 Broadway
Denver, CO 80203
(303) 777-8700
www.eronjohnsonantiques.com
Antique table lamps, wall sconces, candelabra and chandeliers.

Lampa + Möbler
8317 Beverly Boulevard
Los Angeles, CA 90048
(323) 852-1542
Modern and contemporary fixtures.

Luis Baldinger & Sons, Inc.
19-02 Steinway
Long Island City, NY 11105
718-204-5700
Distributor of Bestlite.

TEXTILES & WALLPAPER

Frette
799 Madison Avenue
New York, NY 10021
(212) 988-5221
Elegant linens.

Garnet Hill
www.garnethill.com
Bedding, linens, and home accessories.

Hinson & Co.
979 Third Avenue
New York, NY 10022
(212) 688-5538
Fabrics and wall coverings.

Peter Fasano, Ltd.
964 South Main Street
Great Barrington
MA 01230
(413) 528-6872
Antique and contemporary textiles.

Portico Bed & Bath
212-579-9500
www.porticohome.com
Fine linens and luxury beds.

Smith + Noble
(800) 560-0027
www.smithandnoble.com
Custom-made window treatments, rugs, slipcovers, and duvet covers.

Thibaut
480 Frelinghuysen Avenue
Newark, NJ 07114
(800) 223-0704
www.thibautdesign.com
Specialty wallpapers.

Yves Delorme
www.yvesdelorme.com
Sophisticated linens.

PAINT

Janovic
1150 Third Avenue
New York, NY 10021
(800) 772-4381
www.janovic.com
Quality paints.

Old Fashioned Milk Paint Company
(478) 448-6336
www.milkpaint.com
Paints made from natural pigments.

Pratt and Lambert Historic Paints
www.prattandlambert.com
150-year-old producer of top of the line paints.

picture credits

Foster House, designed by Dave Coote and Atlanta Bartlett
Available for photographic location hire from
www.beachstudios.co.uk
Tel: + 44 (0)1797 344077
Pages 1–2; 10; 16 below; 29 above; 40–41 above and below left; 52–53 above and middle; 70 right; 71; 73 below; 115 above; 142–143; 146–147; 151.

Marina Coriasco
Pages 3; 27; 32; 33 below; 34–35; 36 below; 37; 46; 67 right; 74 right; 89; 110 below; 111; 119; 128; 150.

The family home of Katie and Alex Clarke, owners of boutique hotel The George in Rye
The George in Rye
98 High Street
Rye
East Sussex TN31 7JT
Tel: + 44 (0)1797 224114
www.thegeorgeinrye.com
Pages 4 left; 5 right; 82–83; 104–105; 132; 133 left; 145 left.

A family home in Lydd, Kent
Pages 4 right; 11; 60 below; 70 left; 73 centre; 74 centre; 76; 84; 85 below; 114; 115 below; 160.

Polly Kelly's family home Rose Villa
Available for photographic location hire from
www.georgiancountryhouse.co.uk
Pages 5 left; 5 centre; 8–9; 55; 56 below; 57 below right; 59 above; 59 centre; 64; 65 above and below; 66; 67 left; 72; 73 above left; 107 above right and below; 134 left and above right; 149 below.

The family home of Azzi and Dan Glasser in North London
INA Crystals Ltd
24 Rochester Square
London NW1 9SA
Tel: +44 (0)20 7284 2112
available from
www.liberty.co.uk
Pages 7 above left; 96; 138–139.

Designer Lisette Pleasance and Mick Shaw's home and B&B
Boonshill Farm B&B
Grove Lane
Iden, near Rye
East Sussex TN31 7QA
www.boonshillfarm.co.uk
Pages 7 above right and below left; 16 above; 36 above; 54; 57 below left; 74 left; 102–103; 120–121; 137; 140; 144 and 145 right; 148–149 above.

The home of stylist Twig Hutchinson in London
www.twighutchinson.com
Pages 7 below right; 17; 25 left; 26; 59 below; 78–79; 88; 98 right and 99; 126–127; 141 above.

The family home of the stylist Anja Koops and chef Alain Parry in Amsterdam
Alain Parry's restaurant:
www.Balthazarskeuken.nl
Anja Koops fashion and interior styling:
Anjakoops@hetnet.nl
Pages 12; 18–20; 21 below and 22; 23 below; 33 above; 38; 45 right; 92–93; 95 above; 98 left; 112–113; 124–125; 130 above; 141 below; 152; 157.

Stansfield Road, designed by Dave Coote and Atlanta Bartlett
Available for photographic location hire from
www.beachstudios.co.uk
Tel: +44 (0)1797 344077
Pages 13–15 left; 24; 25 below right; 28 left and centre; 30 right; 39 right; 47; 56 above; 60 above; 61; 69; 85 above and 86 left; 106; 116–117; 129 below; 135.

Anna Parker
P + P Interiors
Tel: +44 (0)7956 404 565
parkerminor@aol.com
Pages 15 right; 30 left; 48–49; 53 below; 65 centre; 90–91; 107 above left; 134 below right.

The home of Zoe Ellison, the owner of i gigi General Store in Hove, Sussex
i gigi General Store
31a Western Road
Hove
East Sussex BN3 1AF
Tel: +44 (0)1273 775257
Email:
igigi@igigigeneralstore.com
www.igigigeneralstore.com
Pages 21 above; 28 right; 42–43; 57 above; 75; 77; 86 right; 108 and 109 left; 122–123; 129 above right.

The home of graphic designer Vanessa van Dam (www.vanessavandam.nl) and Diederik Martens (founder of www.twones.com)
Architecture by www.van-brussel-architectuur.nl
Pages 23 above; 39 centre; 50.

Zwier and Chantal's home in Amsterdam
Pages 25 above right; 29 below; 41 below right; 51.

The Brighton home of Heather Gratton
Heather Gratton
Interior Design and Consultant
www.2refresh.com
info@2refresh.com
Pages 31; 62; 87; 109 right; 133 right; 136.

The house of stylist and designer Ulrika Lundgren of Rika Rikaint B.V.
Oude Spiegelstraat 9
1016 BM Amsterdam
The Netherlands
Tel: +31 20 330 1112
Email: rika_sales@mac.com
www.rikaint.com
Pages 39 left; 58; 63 right; 80–81; 94–95 below; 129 above left.

Anna and John Carver
www.cunning.com
Pages 44 and 45 left; 63 left; 97; 100–101; 118; 130 below and 131; 153.

The stylist Sally Conran's family home in west London
Sally Conran – Interior Stylist
T: +44 (0)20 8451 5667
M: 07980240 967
Page 68.

A private house in Amsterdam owned by Ank de la Plume
www.householdhardware.nl
Page 110 above.

index

acknowledgments

Firstly I would like to thank Polly Wreford for taking such gorgeous pictures… again! Her sharp eye and creative energy know no bounds. Thanks also to Sarah Markillie, Polly's assistant, for all her help and enthusiasm.

A huge thank you goes to all the friends and house owners who allowed us into their homes to take photos. In particular, thanks to Anna Carlos and John Carver, Katie and Alex Clarke, Gabby Eager and Russell Icke, Sally Conran and Twig Hutchinson. Thanks to Samantha Anderson for keeping us well fed, to Michelle Cummings for all her indispensable hard work, and to Stef Stevens-Wade for her help compiling the list of stockists. A very special thank you goes to Helen Ridge (Nellie) and Karena Callen for all their encouragement and kind words – I couldn't have done it without them.

Thanks to everyone at Ryland, Peters and Small for the opportunity and in particular to Alison Starling, Leslie Harrington, Megan Smith, Jess Walton and Annabel Morgan for having such insight and faith in the project.

Finally I would like to thank all my family: my mother, Sasha Waddell, and my father, Stephen Bartlett, for all their creative inspiration and, of course, my three wonderful and amazing sons, Indigo, Hogarth and Bluey, for sacrificing so much mummy time during their summer holidays. Last, but certainly not least, I want to thank Dave, my beautiful husband and partner in life. Surely I must be the luckiest woman alive…